# Powerful and Prayerful Pulpits

# POWERFUL AND PRAYERFUL PULPITS

## FORTY DAYS OF READINGS

## E. M. BOUNDS

Edited by Darrel D. King

BAKER BOOK HOUSE
Grand Rapids, Michigan 49516

© 1993 by Baker Books
a division of Baker Book House Company
P.O. Box 6287, Grand Rapids, MI 49516-6287

ISBN: 0-8010-1034-9

Second printing, April 1995

*Printed in the United States of America*

# Contents

# Preface

IT is from the writings of the assistant editor of the *Christian Advocate* of the general organ of the Methodist Episcopal Church, South, that this volume is comprised. These are jewels that have been locked away in a treasure chest. Each one shines with holy life for every person who will read, receive, prayerfully consider, and embrace it.

This volume is addressed to pastors. Though it will be enlightening and edifying for the whole church, I have assembled the articles that would be primarily of interest to pastors. It is appropriate that these jewels would be in the treasure chest of E. M. Bounds for his beloved fellow pastors throughout the ages. His was a heart of compassion for fellow pastors. He wept for the cities of the nation, he travailed for the churches in America and around the world, his heart was touched by evangelical churches coast to coast and around the world. Dr. Bounds shares with men of God from the heart of a man of God. Open this treasure chest and examine the jewels therein.

I wish to express sincere gratitude, appreciation, and love for co-laborers that helped me so diligently in this project: Kathy Summers, typist; Jenny Powell, free-lance writer and editor, Atlanta, Georgia; and Hazel Luna, librarian, United Methodist, Nashville, Tennessee. I would also like to express my appreciation for their encouragement to Rev. Chester Estes Jr., director of Prayertime Ministries, Union, Mississippi; Rev. James Hamlett, pastor of West Side General Baptist Church,

St. Louis, Missouri; Dr. Ben Rogers, professor at Luther Rice Seminary; and Mike Gibson of Atlanta, Georgia.

A very special thanks to Jan, my wife, and to Beth and Sara, our daughters, for their sacrifice of my time with them.

Yours for revival in this generation.

Darrel D. King, director
E. M. Bounds School
of Prayer and Revivalism

# A Biography of E. M. Bounds

Then He said to me, "Son of man, stand on your feet that I may speak
with you!" And as He spoke to me the Spirit entered me and set me
on my feet; and I heard Him speaking to me. Then He said to me,
"Son of man, I am sending you to the sons of Israel, to a rebellious
people who have rebelled against Me; they and their fathers have
transgressed against Me to this very day. And I am sending you to
them who are stubborn and obstinate children; and you shall say to
them, 'Thus says the Lord God.' As for them, whether they listen or
not—for they are a rebellious house—they will know that a prophet
has been among them. And you, son of man, neither fear them nor
fear their words, though thistles and thorns are with you and you sit
on scorpions; neither fear their words nor be dismayed at their presence, for they are a rebellious house. But you shall speak My words
to them whether they listen or not, for they are rebellious."

[Ezek. 2:1–7 NASB]

THE prophet of prayer was born to Thomas Jefferson (T. J.)
and Harriet Saphronia Bounds. In a small log cabin beside the
banks of the Salt River in Marion County, Missouri, the crying
voice of Edward McKendree Bounds was first heard on August
15, 1835.

During his first year, the family of E. M. Bounds moved and
helped establish the new county of Shelby. The Bounds family's
influence became evident right from the start. T. J. Bounds sur-
veyed Shelbyville, the county seat, and he became a leading
figure in the social, economic, and religious fiber of the town,
which was nestled in the rolling hills of northeastern Missouri.

E. M. Bounds had a secure childhood in the little town of
Shelbyville. When E. M. was 15 years old, his father died and

left his family financially stable and living in a prosperous community.

With his older brother, Charles, E. M. decided to go to California to profit from the great gold rush of 1849. After spending a year in the El Dorado canyon area, the Bounds brothers traveled north and finally returned to Missouri. They returned without success in the gold rush, but the experience strengthened their Christian character.

Before long, E. M. Bounds began studying law. During this time, a great spiritual awakening swept across the United States. In that time of spiritual bliss, E. M. Bounds felt the call to ministry. Abandoning his law practice and embracing the heavenly call, he attended seminary in Palmyra, Missouri. His ministry began in 1859 when he presented himself to the Methodist Episcopal Church, South, Conference in Missouri. On trial, he was assigned the Monticello circuit north of Hannibal. The following year he was assigned to an influential church in Brunswick, Missouri. This church was being pastored at the time by the famous W. G. Caples. As this great man was being assigned to another location, he brought E. M. Bounds to pastor his church. Bounds came to his new pastorate, just as the northern region of Missouri was being ravaged by the escalating Civil War. With the occupation of the Union forces, the fighting of the Confederate forces, and the plundering of the renegades, the populace of this region was being raped, plundered, and abused. In the midst of this chaos, Bounds was arrested and accused of being a Confederate sympathizer. Because he would not swear allegiance to the Union or post bond, Bounds was incarcerated and moved to St. Louis to serve time during the harsh Missouri winter. He spent the Christmas of 1862 incarcerated and abused, but after two weeks in the Gratiot Street prison, he was officially exiled from Missouri by General Curtis, never to return as long as there was conflict.

Eventually he was moved by Union forces to Memphis, Tennessee. He was sent to Washington, Arkansas, where he was released. He then traveled to Jacksonville, Mississippi, and walked more than one hundred miles to Camp Pritchard where he was sworn in as a Confederate chaplain, joining forces with Dr. Sterling Price, a Christian friend and neighbor from Brunswick. On May 13, 1863, he was assigned the chaplaincy of the Missouri Third Infantry. He served in this capacity, not only with the Missouri Third but with other divisions. Reports spread of his effectiveness in bringing spiritual influence to the camps. While traveling with the forces, as the troops would bivouac, he would find a place to preach, often in neighboring churches. At each place, God would move mightily in revival and conversions. This continued even into the trenches at the siege of Vicksburg, Mississippi, and Atlanta, Georgia. Here the intensity of revival was such that it influenced General John B. Hood. He and nine of his officers were confirmed in St. Luke's Episcopal Church. Bishop Henry Law presided over the service and the pastor, Dr. Charles Quintard, assisted.

After the fall of Atlanta, General Hood made a desperate thrust toward Nashville. Great tragedy struck the troops in Franklin, Tennessee. The blood of gallant men mingled on the battlefield where the Missouri forces were so ravaged that they could no longer fight as a strong force. When the battle in Franklin ended, Bounds, though wounded, remained with the casualties to try to help them in their agony and pain. The forces moved on to Nashville in a failed attempt to take it from Union forces, and when the Confederate troops moved back through Franklin in retreat, Bounds came to a decision to stay with the casualties, even though this decision would inevitably lead to his capture and incarceration.

After a six-month incarceration in Nashville, Bounds could not get Franklin off his mind and heart. He returned to the ravaged town where the populace had been decimated by the war. They had given the last of their food, clothing, and hospitality to the soldiers in that tragic battle. Bounds returned to a little church whose members had been scattered. He began to pray and sing praises to God and, as a hen with her chicks, drew the people back together. Before long, they began to grow into a vibrant church.

After a successful pastorate in Franklin, Bounds was called to serve in Selma, Alabama. In a community where he had preached as a chaplain, he now came as the pastor. Here again God poured out his blessings, not only on the Word of God but also on the man of God. Church Street Methodist Episcopal Church, South, where Bounds was pastor, took on a vibrancy tinged with great expectancy. After three years, he was moved from Selma to Eufaula, Alabama, to commence a work in another struggling church. A relocation of the church was required and Bounds led that great church to build a building with a steeple so high that it became the testimony of God's faithfulness to southeast Alabama and the southwest region of Georgia.

He met his first wife, Emmie E. Barnett, while pastoring the Methodist Episcopal Church, South. After four years, he was asked by Bishop Marvin in the St. Louis Conference to pastor the St. Peter's Methodist Episcopal Church, South, in the rapidly growing city of St. Louis, Missouri. He returned to his beloved home state to pastor this church. After four years, Bishop Marvin asked him to pastor the First Methodist Episcopal Church, South, which he did for one year. He came with a high pietistic standard, a clear declaration of God's Word, an example to be emulated, and a power that moved the church to return to the moorings that had built that great testimony in the heart of St. Louis. Bounds then returned to St. Peter's Methodist Episcopal Church, South, and continued his ministry. During this pastorate, after ten years of marriage, God took home his beloved Emmie and left him with two daughters and one son. Harriet Barnett, Emmie's cousin, later became Bounds's wife and his helpmate throughout his remaining years.

While pastoring in St. Louis, he was asked to serve as associate editor of the *St. Louis Christian Advocate* of the Methodist Episcopal Church, South, in Missouri. In this position he became a leader in calling the people of God back to God, not only among the Methodists but among others who read his editorials. He also traveled throughout the region, speaking and preaching in conferences and meetings, impacting churches and communities.

As his reputation for his pietistic stand spread, it was noted in the Methodist Episcopal Church, South, Conference. On May 22, 1890, Bounds was elected to become associate editor of the *Christian Advocate* in Nashville. This national paper for the Methodist Episcopal Church, South, had an impact on all churches that subscribed to it. He served effectively, boldly, and strongly his beloved Methodist Episcopal Church, South, authoring numerous articles that impacted churches of that day. As a prophet, Bounds had followers and detractors. There were those who had ears to hear, who listened and complied, and those who did not hear and became alienated and resentful toward Bounds.

A great revivalist once said that you either receive and respond to a prophet or you destroy him. So it was with Bounds. As he stood with a strong pietistic conviction of righteousness, opposition began to grow. The opposition did not come fully against Bounds but was evident among Christians in political, worldly, and merchandising attitudes that he could not and would not condone. During the national Methodist Episcopal Church, South, conference in Memphis in 1894, Bounds left because of his convictions. Upon returning to Nashville, he concluded his responsibilities there and then moved to his wife's home in Washington, Georgia.

In this beautiful antebellum community, Bounds continued an itinerant revival ministry. It was not Methodist leaders who came to Washington but men of humble hearts, desiring to know God in a righteous piety who came to this great man of God and sat at his feet. Many pastors called him to minister to their flocks, and his ministry of writing continued. At the conclusion of many hours in prayer, he would jot down a few

notes on paper. Finally he produced a first volume called
*Preacher and Prayer.* Other volumes followed.

On August 24, 1913, the voice that rang so loud in the valleys
of Missouri was silenced on earth in the mountains of Georgia,
to be activated in glory to praise Holy God, to magnify the Lord
Jesus Christ, and to embrace the Holy Spirit. Even after his
death, a dear friend, Dr. H. W. Hodge, worked diligently with
the little pieces of paper, paragraphs, and articles and continued
to assemble volumes that have become a library on prayer and
spiritual matters.

# Part One

# 1

# The Preacher: His Power
## *June 21, 1890*

THE preacher is called and commissioned by God. The voice of this divine call must be deep in his soul, the sense of this commission a constant stimulant. Without these the coldness of a profession, the deadness of routine, and the inspiration of self will deprave the preacher and his preaching.

The preacher's vocation will not end while a single soul remains to be ripened for heaven or while the warfare against sin is to be waged. Not till the angel, with one foot on sea and one on land, with uplifted hand and oath, arrests time and dissolves it into eternity, shall the preacher's vocation end, his commission be canceled. Preaching can have no substitute or rivals; to discount or retire it is to discount and retire God.

The power of preaching lies in the divine anointing on the man. Day by day, hour by hour, as his hands and heart are filled with toil, the preacher must be able to say, with a realized consciousness and a glad and buoyant heart, "The Spirit of the Lord God is upon me; he hath anointed me to preach the gospel." This is his consecration and qualification. Though he may have the tongue and wisdom of men and of angels, the power lies in the continuous anointing of the Spirit. The pressure and power of that mysterious Spirit who molded into order and beauty the world and whose hand holds it in its consecrated and stable orbit, must give unction, consecration, and qualification to the preacher. How forceless in the interests of eternal life is the ministry on whose head this divine anointing has never come! The lips that do not glow with the kindlings of this divine flame are impotent to speak for God.

The power of preaching lies in the fact that it sows the life-giving, imperishable seed of God's Word. Only the Word of God has this life-giving energy. Beautiful thoughts, fine sentiments, striking and true statements of philosophy, poetry, or genius have no life of God in them. The preacher may gain reputation, popularity, and influence by these, but the power to quicken and convict consciences, to perfect holiness, and colonize heaven —to do what God designs the preacher to do—will depend on his trueness to God's Word. The more simply and earnestly the preacher becomes the mouthpiece of God, the more diligently he feeds on the Word of God by meditation and prayer and gives it out as the mother gives out her life to her babe, the more his legitimate power will be enhanced. Too often modern preachers know too many books better than they know the Bible and are more alive to the words of man than to the words of God. These have the power of man's words, which is sometimes a strange, marvelous, and beautiful power, but are powerless against sin and powerless to perfect holiness.

The preacher does not scatter pearls but seed of heavenly vitality. The written word of God has been electrotyped on his own soul, has been taken up into his blood and bones, and he gives it out as the soil of Sardinia is said to give out its bitterness at every pore. The pulpit must give forth the word incarnated with life-giving energy, surcharged with the imperishable potencies of God and eternity. The pulpit is debauched when the scholar, the poet, or the orator pose there with brilliant sayings, rhymes, or rhetoric.

The power of preaching lies in the strength of the preacher's faith. Faith is the mightiest and among the rarest of principles. Much of that which goes current as faith by a close spiritual analysis, would be found to contain but a small ingredient of that precious article. Faith does the mightiest things, it has no limit but omnipotence. The roll of its results recorded in Hebrews is without parallel, and these results are to be more.

The preacher must believe with a mighty faith, a faith that is never disturbed by fear, never darkened by a doubt; a faith that never sees the seen but fills its eye and heart with the unseen and eternal; a faith that sees nothing but God, seeks nothing but God, believes nothing but God; a faith that makes the unseen things the real things and counts the seen as low, distrustful, and perishing. Christ said, "He that believeth on me, the works that I do shall he do also; and greater works than these shall he do; because I go unto my Father" (John 14:12). A saying like this lays down the gauntlet and challenges the utmost energies of our faith, and yet to many a pulpit this saying has no fertilizing or miracle-producing stimulant. In the presence of such promised results from faith, how empty our hands! How weak our faith! The limitless powers of faith belong to the pulpit as its endowment. How we need to learn anew the lesson that all things are possible to him that believes and begin in earnest diligence to cultivate faith until it flourishes in exuberant fullness.

The power of the preacher lies in the power of prayer, in his ability to pray so as to reach God and bring great results. The power of prayer is rarely tested, its possibilities seldom understood, never exhausted. The pulpit fixed and fired with holy desires that presses these desires on God with a tireless faith will be the pulpit of power. Nothing is so feeble, so insipid, so nonproductive as a little tedious praying. To pray over our sermons in the same way as we say grace over our meals does no good. Every part of the sermon should be born of the throes of prayer; its beginning and end should be vocal with the plea and song of prayer. Its delivery should be impassioned and driven by the love from the furnace of prayer. Prayer, on fire with intense desire and urged by a faith that does not fold its wings till God is reached, is the mightiest of forces. Prayer that carries heaven by storm and moves God by a resistless advocacy makes the pulpit a throne and its deliverances like the decrees of destiny. The power of preaching must always be backed by a Christlike life. The preacher's every act must be a sermon, his life the Bible illustrated, his holiness pure, the whitest flame. In the manner, measure, or grade of his utterances, no semblance of the world can be found, no points of worldly contact or stain. The life he lives must be the life of heaven on earth. The preacher comes to this position at a great cost, a costly death; but he comes to it, or he doesn't come to its power.

# 2

# Revolutionizing Preachers
## *August 18, 1890*

GOD is in a great strait for men of the right sort. "The eyes of the Lord run to and fro throughout the whole earth, to show himself strong in the behalf of them whose heart is perfect toward him" (2 Chron. 16:9). So spake God's prophet; so might every prophet of God speak down to this hour. God is dependent on men to get into this world, with saving efficacy. His revelations now are incarnate. God is not so careful about numbers as about quality. Numbers alone cannot atone for the lack of quality, but quality may atone for the lack of numbers. It is volunteers that God is looking for. Many people are eager to go. Bishop Thoburn had one hundred volunteers for India, but the searching of his devout and practiced eye sifted them down to three. God wants elect men, men out of whom self and the world have gone by a severe crucifixion—by a bankruptcy that has so totally ruined self and the world that there is neither hope nor desire of recovery—men who by this insolvency and crucifixion have turned toward God perfect hearts.

God found one of the men he was looking for in David Brainerd, whose name and work have gone into history. No sublimer story has been recorded in earthly annals than that of David Brainerd; no miracle attests with diviner force the truth of Christianity than the life and work of such a man. Alone in the savage wilds of America and struggling day and night with a mortal disease, he was unschooled in the care of souls and had access to the Indians for a large portion of time only through the bungling medium of a pagan interpreter. But with the Word of God in his heart and in his hand, his soul fired with the divine flame, and a place and time to pour out his soul to God in prayer, he fully established the worship of God among the Indians and secured all its gracious results. The Indians were released from an ignorant and debased heathenism and became pure, devout, intelligent Christians. All vice was reformed, the external duties of Christianity were at once embraced and acted on, family prayer was set up, the Sabbath was instituted and religiously observed, and the internal graces of religion were exhibited with growing sweetness and strength.

The reason for these results is found in David Brainerd himself, not in the conditions or accidents or God's peculiar election but in the man Brainerd. He was God's man, for God first and last and all the time. God could flow unhindered through him. The omnipotence of grace was neither arrested nor straitened by the conditions of his heart; the whole channel was broadened and cleaned out for God's fullest and most powerful passage, so that God with all his mighty forces could come down on the hopeless, savage wilderness, and transform it into his blooming and fruitful garden; for nothing is too hard for God to do if he can get the right kind of man to do it with.

Brainerd lived the life of holiness and prayer. His diary is full and monotonous with the record of his seasons of fasting, meditation and retirement. The time he spent in private prayer amounted to many hours daily. "When I return home," he said, "and give myself to meditation, prayer and fasting, my soul longs for mortification, self-denial, humility, and divorcement from all the things of the world." "I have nothing to do," he said, "with earth but only to labor in it honestly for God. I do not desire to live one minute for any thing which earth can afford."

Men of this spirit and power are the crowning glory of the gospel, its crying need, its exacting demand. Methodism has stressed this need, her successes have been won by men of this spirit. While not ignoring the incidentals, Methodism had demanded that this one feature of holiness should be central and commanding in her ministry. Her demands on this line are epitomized in the statement of an eminently saintly Scottish preacher: "It is not great talents God blesses so much as great likeness to Jesus. A holy minister is an awful weapon in the hand of God." One of Wesley's Conferences gives this unfailing remedy to revive decayed churches:

> Let every preacher read carefully the life of David Brainerd. Let us be followers of him as he was of Christ in absolute self-devotion, in total deadness to the world, and in fervent love to God and man. Let us but secure this point, and the world and the devil must fall under our feet.

Three men—Harms, Fletcher, and Brainerd—transformed the whole face of things for God, by the power of a faith that deadened them to the world and self and made them alive to God, with a purpose too ardent, too insatiable, too triumphant and forceful to allow division or remission. They are true representatives of God-ordained and God-anointed ministries.

These three men and the conditions they worked in differ in almost every thing, but in what makes for a preacher's success, they are a unit. In deadness to the world, in devotion to God, in absorption in his glory and the salvation of men, in faith, humility, and self-denial, they are one.

We say of them all as Wesley said of one of them in his journal: "I preached and afterward made a collection for the Indian schools in America. A large sum of money is now collected. But will money convert heathens? Find preachers of David Brainerd's spirit, and nothing can stand before them; but without this what will gold or silver do? No more than lead or iron."

# 3

## The Unction
### *October 25, 1890*

In the Christian system unction is the anointing of the Holy Ghost, separating unto God's work and qualifying for it. This unction is the one divine enablement by which the preacher accomplishes the peculiar and saving ends of preaching. Without this unction there are no true spiritual results accomplished; the results and forces in preaching do not rise above the results of unsanctified speech. Without unction the former is as potent as the pulpit.

This divine unction on the preacher generates through the Word of God the spiritual results that flow from the gospel; and without this unction, these results are not secured. Many pleasant impressions may be made, but these all fall far below the ends of gospel preaching. This unction may be simulated. There are many things that look like it. There are many results that resemble its effects, but they are foreign to its results and to its nature. The fervor or softness excited by a pathetic or emotional sermon may look like the movements of the divine unction, but they have no pungent, penetrating, heart-breaking force. No heart-healing balm is there in these surface, sympathetic, emotional movements; they are not radical, neither sin-searching nor sin-curing.

This divine unction is the one distinguishing feature that separates true gospel preaching from all other methods of presenting truth. It backs and interpenetrates the revealed truth with all the force of God. It illumines the Word and broadens and enriches the intellect and empowers it to grasp and apprehend the Word. It qualifies the preacher's heart and brings it to that condition of tenderness, of purity, of force and light that are necessary to secure the highest results. This unction gives to the preacher liberty and enlargement of thought and soul—a freedom, fullness, and directness of utterance that can be secured by no other process.

Without this unction on the preacher the gospel has no more power to propagate itself than any other system of truth. This is the seal of its divinity. Unction in the preacher puts God in the gospel. Without the unction God is absent, and the gospel is left to the low and unsatisfactory forces that the ingenuity, interest, or talents of men can devise to enforce and project its doctrines.

It is in this element that the pulpit more often fails than in any other element. Just at this all important point it lapses. Learning it may have, brilliancy and eloquence may delight and charm, sensation or less offensive methods may bring the populace in crowds, mental power may impress and enforce truth with all its resources; but without this unction, each and all these will be but as the fretful assault of the waters on a Gibraltar. Spray and foam may cover and spangle; but the rocks are there still, unimpressed and unimpressible. The human heart can no more be swept of its hardness and sin by these human forces than these rocks can be swept away by the ocean's ceaseless flow.

This unction is the consecrating force, and its presence the continuous test of that consecration. It is this divine anointing on the preacher that secures his consecration to God and his work. Other forces and motives may call him to the work, but this only is consecration. A separation to God's work by the power of the Holy Ghost is the only consecration recognized by God as legitimate.

The unction, the divine unction, this heavenly anointing, is what the pulpit needs and must have. This divine and heavenly oil put on it by the imposition of God's hand must soften and lubricate the whole man—heart, head, spirit—until it separates him with a mighty separation from all earthly, secular, worldly, and selfish motives and aims, separating him to every thing that is pure and Godlike.

It is the presence of this unction on the preacher that creates the stir and friction in many a congregation. The same truths have been told in the strictness of the letter, but no ruffle has been seen, no pain nor pulsation felt. All is quiet as a graveyard. Another preacher comes, and this mysterious influence is on him; the letter of the Word has been fired by the Spirit, the throes of a mighty movement are felt, it is the unction that pervades and stirs the conscience and breaks the heart. Unctionless preaching makes every thing hard, dry, acrid, dead.

This unction is not a memory or an era of the past only; it is a present, realized, conscious fact. It belongs to the experience of the man as well as to his preaching. It is that which transforms him into the image of his divine master as well as that by which he declares the truths of Christ with power. It is so much the power in the ministry as to make all else seem feeble and vain without it, and its presence atones for the absence of all other and feebler forces.

This unction is not an inalienable gift. It is a conditional gift, and its presence is perpetuated and increased by the same process by which it was at first secured, by unceasing prayer to God by impassioned desires after God, by estimating it, by seeking it with tireless ardor, by deeming all else loss and failure without it.

How and whence comes this unction? Direct from God in answer to prayer. Only praying hearts are the hearts filled with this holy oil; praying lips only are anointed with this divine unction.

Prayer, much prayer, is the price of preaching unction; prayer, much prayer, is the one, sole condition of keeping this unction. Without unceasing prayer, the unction never comes to the preacher. Without perseverance in prayer, the unction, like the manna overkept, breeds worms.

# 4

# Backslidden in the Pulpit
## *November 1, 1890*

MEN have died in the pulpit, but to backslide in the pulpit is more shocking than to die in it. Not so shocking, perhaps, to nerves but far more so to spiritual interests. Many a preacher has backslidden in the pulpit. Spiritual elevation, a forceful commission, and many activities do not provide security against the decline of personal piety. The pulpit in itself is no defense against backsliding. The brain and hands may be busy about the things of God, while the heart is busy about the things of the world. The tongue may be filled with glowing words about religion, and the heart have the chill of spiritual death on it. The busiest man about the duties of the pastorate may be the worst of backsliders. Professional or secular diligence in spiritual things indurates. Mere duty-doing hardens and fossilizes. The spiritual care of others does not insure our religious safety. "They made me the keeper of the vineyards; but mine own vineyard have I not kept." Paul had to be vigilant and busy in his care of others, but his greatest vigilance had to be centered on himself. The hands full of other people's interests may be empty of their own.

Dead, formal routine is both the sign and source of backsliding. When the preacher moves on, by habit and not with heart, by the feeble force of the dying momentum of a past experience or a past call because he is in a rut, the backsliding is a settled fact. The necessity of instituting an investigation to ascertain why his gospel has lost its quickening, converting, edifying force is proof of the regression from first principles and the loss of original power.

When the pulpit is concerned about salary, when money invites or affects it in any way, it is far gone from original righteousness. When the pulpit directs its deliverances to catch the popular ear, when it tones down its awful and solemn truths to the level of a pleasant entertainment, it is a fallen pulpit.

To become worldly is to backslide and the pulpit may be the very school of worldliness. Its deliverances may drip with the foul essence of the lust of the eye, the lust of the world, and the pride of life.

To lose the glow and sensitiveness of religious feeling is to be turning the corner toward backsliding. Intellectual pride is the chronic state of backsliding. Neglecting the devotional reading of the Bible is among the first symptoms of a bad case of pulpit backsliding. Leaving off secret prayer is a strong symptom of a confirmed case.

An orthodoxy that is not freshened and brightened by constant access to the faith and life of the Bible is a backslidden orthodoxy. The pulpit that is not constantly growing in grace and the knowledge of the Lord Jesus is backslidden. The pulpit that is not growing in mightiness, in mellowness, in heavenliness, is on the back track. Old sermons hashed and rehashed, unseasoned by new prayer or new light from God's spirit are symptoms of the disease in a bad form. When new sermons are written in the interest of self to minister to reputation, to secure praise, to enhance popularity, or to please the people the disease has reached its last stages.

# Part Two

# 5

## Words

### *February 7, 1891*

WORDS seem to be little things, easily spoken, and soon die. They pass out of mind and seem to pass out of being. But they are not little things, they are great things; they do not pass out of being, but they pass into being. They preserve our thoughts, shape our tempers, abide in our characters. They hold in form our creeds. Our prayers and praises are set in the framework of words. God is approached by words; they are the offerings of the soul, its intermediary with God. "Take with you words, and turn to the Lord," said the prophet.

Words will be weighty things in the day of judgment. In that great day, "by thy words thou shalt be justified, and by thy words thou shalt be condemned." Words make spiritual character and indicate its perfection. "If any man offend not in word, the same is a perfect man."

As there are good and bad people, so there are good and bad words. The grievous sin of blasphemy is committed by words. The providence of God is arraigned by words; his attributes are inveighed against by words and his majesty dishonored. The unpardonable sin is committed by words. Slander, calumny, backbiting, the long blacklist of evil speaking, is made up of words.

The catalogue of evils is not exhausted by this summary. There are corrupt communications, which are not to be in the mouth nor proceed out of it. There are filthy communications to be avoided. There is foolish talking, random prating, words inflated by vanity and egotism, which must not be named among Christians, such as jesting, which the Bible says is not convenient, and easy, accommodating talking that changes to suit the conditions, like the chameleon its color. Flattery that corrupts both the flattered and the flatterer is done by words.

Then there are idle words that do no good, work no benefit, of which Christ makes the solemn statement that "every idle word that men shall speak, they shall give account thereof in the day of judgment." These weigh against our souls by their very lightness.

Then there are what Paul calls evil communications, words against sound doctrine, words that unsettle faith in the fundamental truths of the Bible; these, he says, corrupt good manners. This kind, he says, eat as doth a canker, they burn into faith and righteousness like a gangrene. An illustration of these cancer words are found in the following incident which appeared lately in a daily paper: "When I was a young girl of fourteen," writes a lady, "I was attending boarding school some distance from home. I was very proud and reticent; so, although nearly heartbroken with homesickness, I did not confide my grief to anyone. Under these circumstances, and while striving with all my heart to be good and truthful in word and deed, I was told to write a composition on 'Truthfulness.' I did my best, writing down every noble and uplifting thought I had, making my composition the honest expression of the belief of a young heart in goodness. The teacher took it for correction, and when she handed it back, she said, with a sneering little laugh, 'That is what we call schoolgirl religion.'" The writer added that she has never since been moved by a high ideal that this mocking laugh has not come back to her.

It is said of Nero, that while young and tender, he regretted that he had learned to write, because he had to sign a death warrant. Many people will, in the day of judgment, wish they had been born dumb when they are confronted with the poisoned fruit of their lips.

There are words that help. It takes strength to comfort in time of death when our hearts and minds are desolate with a great desolation, and yet words do greatly comfort us. "Wherefore comfort ye one another with these words," says Paul. The truth of God coming through the agency of human words is strength, light, and joy in those hours of weakness, darkness, and despair. Behold how great a matter a little fire kindles, and the tongue is a fire. A fire for good, for great good; a fire for evil, for great evil.

# 6

# Edification
### *February 7, 1891*

To edify means to build up. Edification is the scriptural process of perfecting spiritual character. The foundation is laid in conversion, but it takes much toil, cost, and often time to perfect the building; only toiling hearts and hands can mature this divine superstructure. This is the great work of the ministry. The spread of the gospel to every clime is much more dependent on the work of edification at home than superficial Christians are disposed to think. The Church must be made strong by perfecting the character of its individual members or else its advance will be slow and its results unsatisfactory. Christian character is to be matured so that the gospel will have stability and influence, so that it may afford the best specimens of its work to impress and attract, and so that the work it does may be the skill of master workmen.

The main force of New Testament gifts and efforts was turned to this work of edification. Missionaries were sent to carry the news of salvation and plant its seed in other soils, but the permanent spread of the gospel was not dependent on these hurried or itinerant excursions. The edification of believers, their perfection and strength in spiritual character, was the aggressive and attractive force. The Apostle sets forth the matter at length in his letters to the Ephesians, as follows:

> And he gave some, apostles; and some, prophets; and some, evangelists; and some, pastors and teachers; for the perfecting of the saints, for the work of the ministry, for the edifying of the body of Christ: till we all come in the unity of the faith, and of the knowledge of the Son of God, unto a perfect man, unto the measure of the stature of the fullness of Christ: that we henceforth be no more children, tossed to and fro, and carried about with every wind of doctrine, by the sleight of men, and cunning craftiness, whereby they lie in wait to deceive; but speaking the truth in love, may grow up into him in all things, which is the head, even Christ: from whom the whole body fitly joined together and compacted by that which every joint supplieth, according to the effectual working in the measure of every part, maketh increase of the body unto the edifying of itself in love.
>
> [Eph. 4:11–16]

To this object continual reference was made and the whole force of the New Testament church—ministerial, individual, and aggregate—is to work to this end. The zeal of the individual member for spiritual gifts was to be so directed that it might "excel to the edifying of the church." They were charged to "let all things be done unto edifying." They were "to comfort . . . and edify one another." "Our authority," says the apostle, "which the Lord hath given us for edification." The sharpness of apostolic power was to edification. "We do all things, dearly beloved," says Paul, "for your edifying." Conversation was to be only such as was good "to the use of edifying."

# 7

# An Anointed Pulpit
## *May 30, 1891*

AN anointed pulpit is the mightiest agency that God has in this world. It is God's representative, the representative of his holiness, of his power, of his justice, and of his mercy. An anointed ministry is a ministry consecrated and qualified to the great work by the power of the Holy Ghost. This anointing is something more than converting grace, or the grace that enables a preacher to live a pious life. These he receives in common with all true believers. His anointing is separate and above these. It is the added grace by which he is to administer the divinest of institutions. This anointing is part of the call to preach the gospel. The divine call confers the right, the distinguished privilege to preach; the anointing qualifies to preach. The disciples received their call to preach under the personal ministry of Christ; the qualifying power was not received until the pentecostal anointing.

This anointing marks an era in the experience and ministry of the preacher. It is the direct, conscious, and mighty coming of the Holy Ghost on the preacher. His ministry is like another ministry, his gospel like another gospel. It is the gospel clothed in resurrection power and resurrection glory. This anointing comes directly from God. It is the process by which he has his hand on the preacher. It is the channel through which he communicates the irresistible energy of his own fullness and power and by which the preacher empties the full current of God's power on the people. This anointing is the immediate act of God; his movement, his choice, and his application are in it. It is the sign he gives of the right to this royal position as his ambassador. It does not come through ordinances or the laying on of hands, however helpful these may be. It is the personal point of contact between Christ and his disciples. It is their equipment and marching orders. It is to them the signal and the surety of victory.

This anointing is the great promise and blessing of the Christian dispensation; but, like all its promises and blessings, it must be sought after with all the faith, energy, and persistence that its importance demands. It must be sought until all other good is lost sight of, or comprehended in this one of the Holy Spirit. It is to be sought until a new Pentecost is on the heart and tongue, until all the light, life, and power of the Holy Ghost are in the soul. It is to be sought till obtained, and then the retention and increase are to be secured by keeping in full harmony with unselfish aims and high and holy purposes. Divergence from God's aims means the withdrawal of his presence. The failure to cooperate with him dissolves this heavenly partnership. No preacher is ready for his work till he realizes with unquestioned certainty that "the Spirit of the Lord is upon me, because he hath anointed me to preach the gospel."

The ends secured by this divine anointing are twofold: consecration and qualification for the ministry. Consecration is the divine and authoritative setting apart to the ministry, a setting apart that deadens and separates it from all else, that widens by a great exile the preacher's divorce from all secular pursuits and from the pursuits that please and minister to the flesh. It makes of him a spiritual celibate; for Christ only he lives, for Christ only he dies. This is God's way of consecrating his preachers. He puts them with holy hands and holy hearts to the work of God, and shuts their ears and hearts to all the alluring calls from without. No human force can create or enforce this consecration; it must be wrought out, and can only be wrought out, by the energies of the Holy Ghost. The Church may set us apart by its ecclesiastical manipulations, our own choice may lead us to the pulpit—we may be in the ministry as a profession, a vocation, a duty—but these do not constitute consecration to God and his work. The Holy Ghost holds as its own the prerogative to consecrate us. Prophets foretold the coming of Christ, angels announced his advent, obedience to God marked every step of his way, but the Holy Ghost anointed him for his high career.

No instrument but the Holy Ghost can dedicate these powers of ours to God and separate us with a thorough death and a thorough life to the work to which God has called us. What surface, selfish work is done in the name of consecration! How frail and poor the consecration in which resolution and human purposes and promises play the main part! How firm, sustained, complete, zealous, and sweetly loyal is the consecration begotten by the power of the Holy Ghost coming on us in full measure! How unselfish and unworldly, how rich in fruitage is this heaven-compelled and fully accepted consecration! The power to consecrate can be communicated only by the Holy Ghost. We might better say that he is the consecration; where he is in full baptismal force, there is the consecration. We lay our offering on the altar, but the coming of the Holy Ghost is the fire that consumes and sends it in a flame to God. The fire of the Holy Ghost is the only true flame of consecration; the energy of the Holy Ghost is its only force; the presence of the Holy Ghost is its only support and continuance.

The Holy Ghost does not simply consecrate us to an institution or to a pursuit, but he consecrates us to God. This consecration is an evident and conspicuous grace that lifts the preacher and the preaching from the low plane of a profession to that of a divinely attested institution with the credentials of its divinity surcharging the preacher's utterances and glowing in his life and experience. This Holy Ghost consecration puts the man and all he has in the ministry to stir the world for God, backed by all the power of God.

The anointing of the Holy Ghost not only consecrates but qualifies the ministry. Nothing short of the baptism of the Holy Ghost qualifies the preacher. He needs power, the power to raise the spiritually dead, power to deliver from the slavery of Satan, power to enfranchise from the dominion of sin, power to bring the brightness of noonday to the midnight of sin and hell. The power of learning, the power of eloquence, the power of the brain will not qualify for this work. The power of revealed truth is powerless here. The disciples were possessed of all the facts of the gospel before Pentecost, but it took Pentecost to vitalize the truth and enable them to deliver it with saving power. The Holy Ghost descending on the man in power—in its impetuous torrent and its fiery tongues—this is the qualifying power. "Tarry ye in the city of Jerusalem, until ye be endued with power from on high." "Ye shall receive power, after that the Holy Ghost is come upon you." These statements of Christ unfold the secret, the method, and the source of this qualifying power. The pulpit may be clothed with all the elements of human power; it may have influence and attraction from these sources, but if it be not baptized with the Holy Ghost—if all these sources of human power be not discounted, subordinated or surcharged with the power of the Holy Ghost—such a pulpit for the uses of the gospel will be barren and dead.

An anointed pulpit is different from an educated pulpit, though the two may combine if education be crowned with meekness. An anointed pulpit differs from an eloquent one, though this anointing is consistent with the truest eloquence. An anointed pulpit is totally distinct from, if not antagonistic to, an entertaining or sensational pulpit.

An anointed pulpit is a spiritual pulpit. From it the thunder tones of the resurrection life issue: from it the warm and quickening breath of a spiritual spring breathes its life and aroma on the winter of death and sin. From such a pulpit conviction, conversion, and sanctification—all the germinal and edifying processes of the divine life—go forth. An anointed pulpit is a sober pulpit; fearless and true, it deals with God and man's most serious things in a serious way. It deals with delicate and formidable things in a brave and wise way. As the representative of God who is love, the representative of our God who is a consuming fire as well, it reflects God's many facets truly and fully. It defies and molds public sentiment, abhors popular ways, and stands as an ensign of righteousness, truth, and holiness. An anointed pulpit is the most powerful of God's institutions, the tenderest and the firmest, the gentlest and the strongest, the most quieting and the most disturbing, the most attractive and the most repulsive, the best loved and the most hated of things on earth. The one thing that gives God the greatest comfort and gives the devil the greatest trouble—God's great demand, the church's great need—is a pulpit anointed by the Holy Ghost.

# Rules for Preaching
## *August 1, 1891*

IN this day of the multiplication of books on preaching and the burdensome rules laid down, it is refreshing to get hold of something simple, natural, and spiritual by way of direction, and we give as of great value what John Newton wrote to a friend who asked him for rules. "I have formerly fettered myself," he says, "by following other people's rules, and therefore ought not to shackle my friend by prescribing to him. You have the word of grace, the throne of grace, and the Spirit of grace. Under this divine direction, what passes within you and around you will furnish you with better rules for your own management than you could possibly receive from the wisest man upon earth who was not exactly in your situation. Various have been the methods," continues Newton, "my wise and gracious Lord has taken to break down my spirit of self-dependence and to hide pride from me."

If the Lord can but secure this end in us, he can make first-class preachers of any of us. It is not so much the lack of rules, the lack of method or of manner that hinders the best results in preaching, but the self that remains in us and subordinates our duties to its unhallowed uses. When the spirit of pride in all its unnumbered forms and the spirit of self-dependence in its endless diversity are destroyed in us by God's severe discipline and the brightness of his glory fills us, we are more ready to preach the gospel than we are with all the diplomas of all the theological schools in our hands and all the rules of all the preaching books stereotyped within us. Mr. Newton closes with this most important statement: "Of all the maxims I have met with about preaching," he says, "I most admire that of Luther, which is: 'To have prayed well is to have studied well.'"

In closing his letter Mr. Newton says: "If my mind were in a right frame toward the Lord, I think I should not be greatly embarrassed if called to preach at five minutes' warning to the most respectable congregation." No man will ever gain true success as a preacher, however well equipped otherwise, who does not put these spiritual qualifications first and always keep them to the front.

# 9

# Power from on High
### *August 22, 1891*

THE message of Gethsemane and Calvary had to wait for
Pentecost because the facts—the letter without the Spirit—were
dead. The transfiguration, the cross, the blood, the shock of the
resurrection earthquake could not project the gospel. These
forces waited for their crowning glory, the Spirit's fiery tongues.
The power of Christ's dispensation is a fiery pulpit—not a
learned pulpit, not a popular pulpit, not an eloquent pulpit, but
a pulpit on fire with the Holy Ghost! A pulpit may be fired with
unhallowed flames; the fire of popularity, the fire of ambition,
the fire of party, of sect, or of creed may inflame the pulpit, and
much heat of one kind or another may be kindled. Fiery tongues
of this sort will not give vent to the energy of the Holy Ghost.
Only the energy of a false, delusive flame will issue from these.
The true pulpit is God's fire in the world. Its flame is heaven-
kindled; its power the Holy Ghost on the preacher.

This feature of power from on high distinguishes preaching
from all other systems of didactic propagandism. This power
is not the mere iteration or reiteration of truths well learned
or well told, but it is the enabling force to declare revealed truth
with superhuman authority. The preacher must have the power

given by direct connection with God. As the golden pipes transmitted the golden oil in the prophet's vision, so the relation between the preacher and God must be precious and without intermission. The pipes must be kept open; every thing that will in any measure hinder or choke the freest and fullest flow of this divine current must be removed. The pipes must be clean and kept clean. The preacher must empty himself of self, of the world, and of sin, and keep himself perpetually and scrupulously emptied. The unseen and mighty spiritual forces must continually be imparted to him from God, giving divine power to the preacher and his word in a way that is foreign to the utterances of unanointed or secular lips.

The speaker for God may lack all else that gives human lips audience, yet having this power he has that which qualifies him for the work, though it may be unseemly by human estimates and gain but shame to the speaker. Although endued with all the aggregate forces that captivate, convince, and enforce truth or opinions in judgment, if he lacks this power, which is not taught in earthly schools or transferred by human hands or learned by artful rules and which defies rhetoric, taste, and eloquence, his ministry by God's estimate and in spiritual results will fall far below zero.

God does not mix this power with other solutions to give it efficiency. It is not some or much of the Holy Ghost mixed with some or much of other ingredients. This power is from the Holy Ghost singular and alone. It is the one thing to be sought and secured, the one thing whose importance discredits all other things, the one thing that stands alone unrivaled and supreme. The circumstances and dignity of official position, the show of human learning, the vain adornments of a vicious eloquence must be despised in the pursuit of this absolutely essential, all-important thing.

Literary taste, the erudition of science, pleasing mannerisms, secular eloquence, these do not help to clothe the preacher with that unique power that alone can enable him to perform his unique work. These tend, like a luxuriant growth, to dissipate vital forces and abate the harvest fullness.

This power is something distinct from and superior to all forms of human power that may be in the pulpit and which may give it influence. This power is not the force of a mighty intellect, holding in its giant grasp great truths, flooding them with light and forming them into shapeliness and beauty. Neither is this power the effect of great learning, nor is it the result of an address faultless and complete by rule. This power is not held in the keeping of any of these earthly sources of power. The effects and energy of these forces are essentially different in source, character, and result from this power from on high.

It is the transmission of power from God, a bestowal in measure and force of that energy that pertains only to God and is transmitted to the preacher in answer to the waiting, longing, wrestling attitude of his soul before God, conscious of his impotency and seeking God's omnipotence. This power may be found in combination with one or all of the sources of human power but must not be confounded with them and is not dependent on them. Whatever of human force may be present in the preacher, it is not to be trusted in or made conspicuous. The human must be hidden, lost, or inspired by this divine power.

The preachers of the present day excel those of the past in many, perhaps in all, the human elements of success. They are well abreast of the age in learning, profound research, and intellectual vigor; but the presence of these do not insure the gift of power from on high, neither do the largest measure of these—and that in the most commanding and impressive form—in the least abate the necessity for the added and full endowment of the Holy Ghost. Modern preaching seems to fail in the very thing that creates and distinguishes true preaching, and which is essential to its being, and which can only elevate it into a divine and powerfully aggressive agency. It lacks the heavenly unction; it fails as the channel through which God's saving power may thunder on consciences. Modern preaching fails by a lack of that sacred, potent influence, which disturbs the sinner in his sleep of carnal security and awakens by its thunder peals his terror-stricken soul, which quickens and arouses the conscience from its ignoble and fatal stupor, which convulses the will by a mighty revolution, which searches into the secret parts of man's inner being, dividing the joints and marrow, opening the awful and mysterious depths and laying them bare to self and God, and which infuses new blood into the heart and veins of faith and arms it with courage and skill for the battle and the victory. These ends can never be secured by a pulpit clothed only with the human elements of power, however gracious, comfortable, or helpful they may be.

This power from on high is the one element on which God stakes the success of the pulpit, his one supreme condition of success—so supreme as to stand alone as the one universal, enduring, changeless endowment for God's preachers in all ages and among all classes. Without it the pulpit will always be veering between faith and philosophy, always powerless to stem the torrent of sin and worldliness, and will itself flounder in the storm of doubt or infidelity. This power is the only thing that can save the ministry to Christ and his church, the only thing that can save the church through the ministry. The essence of this power cannot be captured by a definition. It eludes description. It is the common inheritance, the indispensable need of every preacher. It is the great promise, the richest provision of Christ's dispensation. But it does not come simply by promise or provision; it is conditional. It must be waited for, sought for, wrestled for until received, realized. This power is not inherent in the Word of God; it does not lie in the facts of the gospel. It is the fire of God that descends on the preacher and gives to these divine facts and truths their dynamic force. This power belongs to the preacher by a conscious divine endowment. It pervades his soul as a fragrant unguent. It is on his head and heart and tongue, exudes through his life, sets tongue and heart on fire, lays soul and body on the altar—God-touched, God-illumined, God-inflamed, God-empowered. By it the whole man is transformed and his utterances become pointed, barbed, and transfixed with convicting force and saving power.

# 10

# The Preacher and Discipline
## *November 24, 1891*

CHRISTIAN discipline has as its end the regulation and perfection of the whole religious character. It has to do with the whole range of influence, motive, habit, association, and condition. It has much to do with the edifying and perfecting of the saints as well as with the pains and penalties from offenders. The entire gospel system is a training school, and discipline is vital to its integrity. The preacher is the representative and the administrator of this discipline. Its efficiency, almost its being, are lodged with him. It belongs to his most unpleasant but most necessary and fruitful work. The experience of Robert McCheyne, one of the holiest, most gifted, and most useful of ministers, in regard to discipline will, to some extent, reflect the attitude of every faithful preacher on the subject.

When I first entered upon the work of the ministry, I was exceedingly ignorant of the vast importance of church discipline. I thought that my great and almost only work was to pray and preach. I saw your souls to be so precious, and the time so short, that I devoted all my time and care and strength to labor in word and doctrine. When cases of discipline were brought before me and the elders I regarded them with something like abhorrence. It was a duty I shrank from; and I may truly say it nearly drove me from the work of the ministry among you altogether. But it pleased God, who teaches his servant in another way than man teaches, to bless some of the cases of discipline to the manifest and undeniable conversion of the souls of those under our care and from that hour a new light broke in upon my mind, and I saw that if preaching be an ordinance of Christ, so is church discipline. I now feel very deeply persuaded that both are of God—that two keys are committed to us by Christ; the key of doctrine, by means of which we unlock the treasures of the Bible; the other the key of discipline, by which we open or shut the way to the sealing ordinances of the faith. Both are Christ's gift, and neither is to be resigned without sin.

Authority is necessary to the exercise of discipline. The preacher has authority—the authority of a divine call, the authority of a divine relation, the authority of a divine word. He is called by divine election to be the spiritual ruler of his people. He is there to govern. Under rule and discipline himself, he is there to exercise the same. The preacher in the pulpit, if rightfully there, is there by divine appointment and there with ability to exercise the prerogatives of this holy spiritual relationship. A thorough realization and deep conviction of his divine call is essential to the right exercise of this authority. If the preacher does not realize his relation as immediate from God he will have low views of the dignity, responsibility, and solemnity of this relationship. He will become a caterer, a professional, or a despot. Authority will be vaguely realized, feebly, coldly, or harshly exercised.

As the ministry loses sight of its original character as a divine institution, clothed with divine power, it loses in a large measure its training force. As it degenerates into a profession or panders to popular tastes or is a manufactory of sensation on a small or large scale, its high authority is surrendered for a vain, fleeting, unholy popularity. The right to exercise authority in the things that pertain to God's church is essential to the ministry. Where the material is rough and hard and the polish to be secured the highest, the transformation to be worked most radical and beautiful, the character to be secured the divinest, then something more than influence, example, or truth, however strong, clear, or benign, must be brought to bear. Power must be there along with the right to exercise that power, which creates authority. The preacher's authority is the divine call to a divine relationship to God's people, backed by a divine word.

The Word of God is surcharged with formative forces. Christ purged and perfected his disciples by his word. The Word of God faithfully proclaimed in its whole counsel has an all-creating, an all-forming force. Its weighty and solemn truths, uttered with ceaseless iteration and reiteration with the energy of the Holy Ghost and all the direct simplicity of a man in dead and most serious earnest about the things of God and eternity, cannot fail to re-create consciousnesses, renew hearts, change heads, and transform lives. They cannot fail to train the hearers in all the elements of a serious and holy character. Such deliverances of God's Word cannot fail to sift and to purge, cannot fail to separate the precious from the vile, in character, association, and condition. The words of the true preacher are ponderous words; they weigh like tons of lead. They are eating words; they burn like caustic. They are sharp words; they cut like a sword or razor edge.

> A two-edged blade,
> Of heavenly temper keen;
> And double were the wounds it made,
> Where'er it glanced between.
> 'Twas death to sin—'twas life
> To all who mourned for sin;
> It kindled and it silenced strife,
> Made war and peace within.

The preacher, to secure the ends of discipline, must be loyal to God's Word. He must have a thorough conviction of the truths of the Bible as the revelation of God, the hearty and full acceptance of its statements as solemn verities. The truths of God's Word believed and experienced by him must be declared in full force without compromise or toning down, without speculation, hesitancy, dubiety, or feebleness. The uses of discipline are destroyed by speculation or by a disputatious or doubtful way of declaring God's truth. The ends of discipline can never be secured by the rhetorician, the studied orator, or the preacher who is seeking for the popular channels or the itching ears. Salary, fame, or anything else in the pulpit but the single eye to God's glory destroys the efficiency of its training.

The preacher must be anointed by the Holy Ghost to secure the ends of discipline. Law, rules, penalties, without the sweetness or oil of this divine unction, have in them too much of law for happy training. The letter kills. The Spirit gives life. Rust or friction will wear out, break, or derail the machinery of unctionless training. The preacher's deliverances without it will be dull, limp, harsh, legal, or passionate.

Pastoral care and visitation are strong elements of discipline. A vigilant and loving eye, searching with tender and solicitous inquisition into the piety of our daily lives, into the privacy of home life, comes in to us with a scrutinizing gaze where we really live, where we are seen in the undress of our true selves. Such tender, jealous care; such watchful, loving anxieties expressed by personal contact in business and home life cannot fail to discipline with a strong, gentle, and ever-pressing hand.

Back of the preaching as a disciplinary force lies the personal character of the preacher. Character carries conviction; character attracts, molds, rules; character has authority in it. Words and principles are weighty when backed by character. The integrity, sincerity, cleanness, and courage of the preacher elevate him to an authority that no brilliance of talents, no oratorical powers, no learning can raise him. An undisciplined character cannot train. It requires discipline to produce disciples. Only disciplined characters can discipline character. A disciplined character is not an austere character. It does not mean severity, by symmetry, solidity, sympathy, and strength. A disciplined character lives the rules he enforces, embodies the principles he declares, illustrates the system he advocates. Rules and law are incarnated in him. They are no longer dry, stern, iron abstractions, but they have become by the touch and presence of the preacher real flesh and blood, living, alluring things. The preacher who makes the rules his drink and meat, his blood and bones, will draw others to the transmuting process; their leanness will hunger for the food upon which the preacher has feasted and been made fat. He who governs himself governs others. He who has conquered himself can conquer others. We can do but little to train others in principles in which we have never been trained. We cannot project molding forces when we have never been fashioned by those forces.

# Part Three

# 11

# What Hinders Preaching

*February 11, 1892*

AMONG the things that hinder spiritual results, fine preaching must have place among the first. Fine preaching is that kind of preaching where the force of the preacher is expended to make the sermon great in thought, tasteful as a work of art, perfect as a scholarly production, complete in rhetorical finish, and fine in its pleasing and popular force. In true preaching the sermon proceeds out of the man. It is part of him, flowing out of his life. Fine preaching separates between the man and the sermon; he may be the architect, he may build the sermon, but the preacher and the sermon are two. More than this it separates between the Holy Ghost and the sermon. Such sermons will make an impression, but it is not the impression that the Holy Ghost makes. Influence it may have, but the influence is not distinctly spiritual, if spiritual at all. These sermons do not reach the conscience, are not aimed at it. Some other part of the nature that is more easily reached and bears more pleasant fruit than an awakened conscience draws the arrow from this polished quiver. The preacher has made too much of the sermon; the sermon has made too much of the preacher; the hearer has made too much of both preacher and sermon for either the Holy Ghost or conscience to make much of either sermon or preacher.

The sermon may convey the truth, may be stalwart in its orthodoxy, but the orthodox truth may be lost in the wealth of fine statement. Two things are requisite to secure spiritual results for the sermon: It must be God's revealed truth, and that truth must be stated in such a way as to secure the attendance of the Holy Ghost. To accomplish this there must be simplicity and directness of statement coupled with fine-sighted aim at the conscience. The least addition of self or the least insincerity, putting anything to the front, to the rear, or in the middle but God's glory, will arrest the flow of the Spirit.

God's plan in regard to preachers and preaching confounds all human wisdom, opposes our views, violates our tastes, offends our pride, and staggers our faith. It is that

> God hath chosen the foolish things of the world to confound the wise; and God hath chosen the weak things of the world to confound the things which are mighty; and base things of the world, and things which are despised, hath God chosen, yea, and things which are not, to bring to nought things that are: That no flesh should glory in his presence. . . . That, according as it is written, He that glorieth, let him glory in the Lord.
>
> [1 Cor. 1:27–29, 31]

This method that seems to directly oppose the fitness of things, this passing by the showy agencies of this world, was not a matter of chance or because God was in a strait, but this was God's deliberately chosen and settled plan. The reason is that the agencies of this world are so unfit to secure the great results. No glory would accrue as a result of these agencies, but to those things fit for God, all glory is referred at once. Paul's own commission to preach is illustrative of the same great principles. Christ, he says, sent me "to preach the gospel: not with wisdom of words, lest the cross of Christ should be made of none effect." God negated Paul's fine preaching in the words of his commission. Fine preaching destroys the power of the cross. Its edge and force are bandaged and broken by garlands. The beauty and fitness of things coffins the cross. Paul's ministry was true to his commission. He declares:

> And I, brethren, when I came to you, came not with excellency of speech or of wisdom, declaring unto you the testimony of God. For I determined not to know anything among you, save Jesus Christ, and him crucified. And I was with you in weakness, and in fear, and in much trembling. Any my speech and my preaching was not with enticing words of man's wisdom, but in demonstration of the Spirit and of power: that your faith should not stand in the wisdom of men, but in the power of God.
>
> [1 Cor. 2:1–5]

"His bodily presence [was] weak and his speech contemptible" to the lettered Greek. Self-distrust and self-emptying marked his ministry. It is amazing how much of self can be crammed into one sermon. Paul's statement rejects fine thoughts, fine rhetoric, and all methods of philosophical dealing with the gospel. He rejects all methods of cultured speech, which would have secured reputation to himself and made his preaching popular among the elegant Greeks. All these he rejected as vicious alloy hindering the demonstrations of the Holy Ghost and destroying faith.

Mr. Wesley said he dared not preach a fine sermon. He says of his sermons, "Nothing here appears in an elaborate, elegant, or oratorical dress. I design plain truth for plain people."

Robert Hall said in his later ministry: "My strain of preaching is considerably altered; much less elegant, but more intended for conviction, for awakening the conscience, and carrying home truths with power to the heart." Savonarola said of a very popular preacher: "These verbal elegancies and ornaments will have to give away to sound doctrine simply preached." Robert McCheyne cried out in prayer: "Enlarge my heart and I shall preach." His biographer says: "In this remark we see the germ of his remarkably solemn ministry: he gave out not merely living waters, but living waters drawn at the spring he himself had drank of. Others try a more intellectual method, but as the intellect is not the part of the discourse which lodges an arrow in the conscience, this intellectual preaching must have tenfold more prayerfulness bestowed on it, it if affect the heart of either the preacher or the people." This increased prayerfulness is the very thing this fine preaching does not have. The men of preaching hearts are the only preachers of prayerful hearts. When so much force is spent on the literary, intellectual, and artistic part of the sermon, very little is spent in prayer. The reliance is on influences other than that of the Holy Ghost coming through prayer to give the sermon the desired popular results.

The wisdom of words, even their persuasive beauty, abate the power of the gospel. The ends of the gospel cannot be secured by oratory, by rhetoric, by logic, by any kind of tasteful, scholarly statement. More than that, these detract from the essential effects of the gospel, and if the true ends of the gospel are not wholly lost by this "excellent speech" or these "enticing words," the results are enfeebled and reduced to a losing minimum. Christ did not choose orators, philosophers, rabbis, or scribes, to preach his gospel. He chose unlearned, common men of common education with common talent and common sense. The gospel is not to be propelled by intellect but by heart. The Holy Ghost resides not in the intellect but in the heart.

A statement of this kind is not to be used in the defense of either ignorance or laziness. No man ought to be wiser than God's preacher: wise in the wisdom that God gives, wise in the wisdom of following God's plan and submitting to and obeying God's will. None should be more learned than he: learned in the things of God, learned in the things of his own heart. None should be more industrious than he, absorbed in God's work and in caring for God's sheep and giving himself "continually to prayer, and to the ministry of the word." None should be a greater student than he, absorbed in studying God's Word, intent on securing that personal nearness and likeness to Christ that will ensure the full measure of success. He will give his life for God's sheep, happy in suffering or doing God's will, incessant in proclaiming God's Word. The preacher will find his time and strength engrossed and will have neither time nor taste for the vanities or glare of secular eloquence. These are a part and portion of that world that he has forsworn. His sermons will flow out of him from the streams, which have flowed into and filled him from the throne of God. They are a part of him, living and not manufactured by square and rule and compass, born from the incorruptible Word of God, which liveth and abideth forever.

The world has never been mightily moved to Christ by the fine sermons or great fame of great preachers. It was when they were despised and without fame that Wesley and Luther did their great work for God, and their greatness and fame were the results of the success won in the fires of persecution, contempt, and scorn. One of the most magnificent of pulpit intellects and orators utters toward the close of his life this lament: "If any saving fruit has been reaped from my ministry it has been almost entirely among the middling and lower classes." Many a lowly Methodist exhorter has far exceeded this in conscious gathered fruit.

# 12

## A Bible Ministry
### *February 25, 1892*

THE Bible does not ask to be vindicated. Its only demand is that it be proclaimed. It requires no bodyguard of critics or scholars for its protection. It does not come into court with advocates to try its case. The Bible pleads its own case. It will vindicate its divine claims, if it can get preachers to proclaim it. The lack of learning and critical skill to defend the Bible may cause the defection of a few brains and the disturbance of faith in some cases, but the preaching of the Bible will confirm faith, convict consciences, and purify hearts everywhere. Men are not to be saved in the first or second instance by thought—original or brilliant—by learning—scholarly or critical—by splendor of diction, nor by perfecting the art of sermon making. Homiletics, criticism, and rhetoric will play a poor part in this war. It is to be fought by the Bible, by Bible preachers and Bible Christians. We would not say that the need of the times is for eloquent, learned, able, or popular preachers, but we believe the greatest need of this age is for Christians who live the Bible, and there cannot be Bible Christians without a Bible ministry. Bible preachers will make Bible Christians. Our need, then, first and foremost, is for men who will preach the Bible in such a way as to make it the sum and substance of their preaching, men who will go through our churches with the Bible, not simply in their hands or under their arms but in their hearts, graven there with a pen of fire. A Bible ministry is one to which the Bible is the best known of all books; it is one that has the whole Bible on the tip of its tongue so that the whole range of its principles, facts, and duties are as familiar as household words. Many preachers are strangers to God's word, not strangers from the standpoint of a student only, or strangers from the standpoint of profound spiritual insight merely, but strangers in the most commonplace way. They know books about the Bible, the country of the Bible they know, but the Bible they do not know. The study of the Bible is very different from studying books about the Bible. The difference is far greater than that between reading books about the sun and seeing its cloudless glory and bathing in its noontide heat and light. A Bible ministry can only be reached by men of simple habits and simple consecration, men with an unworldly and childlike spirit, men who center their ambitionless aim with wholehearted intensity on knowing God's written Word so that they may proclaim it in a way that people can understand it. The Bible itself must be studied without note or comment, studied as no other book can or ought to be studied, studied with the most intense devotion and the most implicit faith in its utterances, studied by the light of God's Spirit, studied with continual and urgent prayer for light and wisdom, studied as God's only infallible and all-sufficient Book, studied as though there were no other book in the world.

A Bible ministry means heart study and heart knowledge of the Bible. There can be no true knowledge of the Bible, no efficient proclamation of it, till it is hidden in the heart with heart-loyal subscription to its truths and its spirit permeates the inner man. The Word of God must be in the preacher's heart as a vital, fruitful force before he can project its power or distribute its seed with skill. No man can know the Bible who does not know it in his heart. The blindest of men are those whose heads are crammed with Bible facts and figures but whose hearts are Bible blanks. A true Bible ministry ministers out of the heart and to the heart. Like his great Antitype, the Bible preacher has the Word incarnated, and can say, "I have given unto them the words which thou gavest me."

This heart knowledge means more than a professional knowledge of the Bible, much more than a critical knowledge of the original languages in which it was written. It means an experience of its truth, which gives the energy of fiery conviction to its utterances. It means that the true Bible ministry is the ministry of a Bible heart, a heart in which Bible principles have become living, experienced, practical truths. It means the ministry of a pure heart, as well as the ministry of Bible principles because no man can see God but through the medium of a pure heart, so no man can know or preach God's word without a pure heart.

A Bible ministry is one that proclaims God's word with unfaltering courage and strict fidelity. Such a ministry shuts itself up to God's Word and does not go outside of it. The times, the popular themes, do not entice. It stands on the Word of God and proclaims it and leaves it to work out its far-reaching ends. Such a ministry does not shun to proclaim the whole counsel of God; distasteful truths are proclaimed with the same fullness and fidelity as those that may have a popular relish. To preach the Bible is not to ignore dogma, for the Bible is the most dogmatic of books, but still the true ministry is not the ministry of creeds or professions but of the Bible. To preach the Bible is much more than going over a system of theology. To preach theology may be good, but the difference between the preaching of a system of theology and preaching the Bible is the difference between watering a country by digging cisterns at stated intervals and filling them with water and watering that country by pouring through it a river fed by living springs, with its ever running and exhaustless life-giving tide.

The Bible ministry does not make the Bible simply a textbook from which a motto is secured or from which cleverness, thought, and taste may bring about a sermon—the Bible giving the text, but the world giving the sermon. The Bible ministry is not a ministry of sermon making, in which the Bible truth is lost in the sermon: a thimbleful of Bible dissolved in a sea of sermon, the proportion going beyond the infinitesimals of homeopathy. The preacher and the sermon are to be saturated, impregnated, and suffused with the substance and the spirit of the Bible; the preacher and the sermon must hold the Bible in solution against precipitating energy.

It was said by a very wise man that the man of one book was to be feared; that is, as an antagonist, as a man of thought and force. The Bible ministry ought to be, in its directness and concentrated energy, the "man of one book." It ought to hold the Bible in high esteem, as though there could be no other book but it, as though it involved all books and all learning.

Mr. Wesley has been distinguished as "the man of one book" in this sense. He says: "My decision is in some sense to forget all that ever I have read in my life. I mean to speak in the general as if I had never read one author, ancient or modern (always excepting the inspired)." His whole ministry had this keynote: "A man of one book." "Give me the Book of God," he says. "At any price give me the Book of God. Here is knowledge enough for me."

The Bible preachers have the successful and powerfully influential ministries. Mr. Moody's influence and career for good find their solution in his loyalty to, and knowledge of, the Bible. He has become the man of practical wisdom and the influential factor in religious work, almost solely from the fact that he has studied the Bible and adhered to its plain, common-sense meaning and delivered its teachings with the earnestness of personal conviction. Mr. Spurgeon was a "man of one book" and had a deathless hold on the truths of that book and preached its truths with strength and conviction. The critics, since his death, have almost without an exception, attributed his success mainly, or in measure, to the fact that he was a Bible preacher. The following criticism from the "Churchman" voices this point:

But of all the qualities that made him and his life a defense of
Christianity was his knowledge and ready application of the Bible,
as containing the inspired word of God, to the lives and needs of ordinary men. The Bible was his oracle, and he made it the oracle of his
hearers. He was a scriptural preacher, a textual preacher. He proved
how potent is the language of the sacred book, how completely it
serves for the guide and inspiration of human lives. There have been
many preachers more learned than Spurgeon, many more original.
The pulpits of America and England have recently sounded forth
much that is gorgeous and convincing, and have echoed the best
examples of the sermon from Chrysostom to Phillips Brooks, but this
century has not heard a voice raised for Christ with so complete a
mastery of scripture thought and language as was exhibited by
Spurgeon, who has left a precedent and an example as a man mighty
in the Scriptures, which no preacher, of whatsoever church or denom-
ination, can afford to disregard.

Few preachers have time or talent to become great scholars,
learned theologians, or eloquent divines; or if they could, life
is too practical, the call of their responsibilities and duties too
weighty, to spend life that way, but all may become Bible
preachers, and thereby fit themselves to do the greatest good.
To be the Word of God was the highest mission of the Son of
God. To minister the Word of God was the sum of apostolic
calling. It is the sum of God's calling to this good day. There
is no more potent regulator of society, no speedier cure for the
ills of the times, no greater promoter of righteousness than a
true Bible ministry. "God has magnified his Word above all his
name." His preachers will be wise if they elevate his Word to
the same lofty and divine eminence.

# 13

## A Serious Ministry
### *March 3, 1892*

A ministry that saves people from sin and prepares them for heaven must be a serious ministry. No light gospel can meet the serious demands of this serious work. The gospel of fun may draw but cannot save, may please but not edify. The gospel never appeals to the fun-loving side of our nature; its work is done by restraining or ignoring the lighter elements and basing its operations on the profound and weighty elements of our being. Christ and his gospel are the most serious expressions of God. It is the gospel of the cross bathed in tears and blood and crowned with death. Christ's gospel can only reach and save by breaking hearts. The first response of a soul to its call is the paleness of guilt and the gall of repentance. Its saving benefits can only be conducted through a sober channel. A serious ministry is not an austere ministry; it is a thoughtful ministry, sobered by responsibility and deep concern, serious because of the grave interests involved—perils as appalling as perdition and as lasting as eternity.

We may criticize and caricature a sour, long-faced religion as it deserves to be; yet, notwithstanding this counterfeit, the genuine article is charged with gravity and meets with prayer and thought the weighty interests involved in this life and in the one to come. While this gospel of ours is removed by an immeasurable distance from the hollow and hard austerities that make piety repulsive, it is removed still farther from the spirit of levity, which reduces the whole matter, or any part of it, to a joke. We are at this time in far greater danger from the gospel of fun than we are from the gospel of vinegar. Austerity and humor, though in different ways, are non-conductors—the one is too icy and hard, the other is too volatile and porous. The Holy Ghost never flows through the channel of a laugh. Conviction, prayer, and frivolity do not mix. December's ice is not more destructive to flowers than a light and careless spirit is to all the graces of the Spirit. All these serious frames are the very things to be begotten by the ministry, and these gracious ends cannot be secured but by a serious ministry. The vast amount of surface piety current among us is owing in the main to the lack of serious preaching. The great truths that arrest, sober, and stir are ignored by the surface and popular pulpit; the weighty and alarming facts of the gospel are dismissed to give place to the superficial, showy, and transient. The elements of a thoughtful, reverent, and devout piety are wanting. The ordinary Christian, as well as the sinner, needs first of all things to be sobered. A serious pulpit will do this. It will make the people feel that they are dealing in verities as solemn as eternity. Seriousness in the pulpit will go far to banish the frivolous feelings, the frivolous talk, and the frivolous conduct, which are so evident in many congregations. The lack of soberness in the pew is generally traceable to lack of seriousness in the pulpit. Church-going people take their cue generally from the preacher, at least this is the case when the cue is one to which they are inclined. Frivolity is the world's gospel. It preaches it all week. God's gospel is at the other end and always charges men to be serious, to stop and to think that the grave is just ahead and eternity is involved. Seriousness is not a popular quality, and this in a measure accounts for its rarity. Its unpopularity and scarcity are loud appeals for its exercise. The pulpit that seeks popular themes, that itches for popularity, will not tolerate seriousness because it throws a damper on popular interests, arrests popular effects, and hinders or dissolves surface piety.

If the prophets, if Christ and his apostles, are to serve as examples, then seriousness and holiness are prerequisite to a true ministry. These were serious men, burdened with heartbreaking burdens—men of tears, of strong cryings, but never men of frivolity or of laughter. Whatever lightness of spirit they had naturally it was sobered in the presence of their grave responsibilities. Christ's ministry was a serious one. He spoke in parables to awaken serious thought. He spoke of the worm that does not die and the fire that is not quenched that he might arrest and sober his listeners. He enjoined silence concerning some of his great works so that no sensation unfavorable to true spiritual results should be excited. Many nights he spent in prayer, often in tears; there is not one expression, not one act, to relieve the deep seriousness, which pervaded his entire ministry.

Paul looked on the world from Christ's standpoint, and to him a ministry to such a world could be nothing else but a serious ministry. His call to it was of such serious import as to banish forever all trivial thoughts about its design or nature. "I take you to record this day, that I am pure from the blood of all men" is a protest that could have no place with a trifler or humorist. His dying charge to Timothy is the condensed seriousness of his own ministry bequeathed as a solemn legacy to all who should follow him:

> I charge thee therefore before God, and the Lord Jesus Christ, who shall judge the quick and the dead at his appearing and his kingdom; preach the word; be instant in season, out of season; reprove, rebuke, exhort with all long-suffering and doctrine.
>
> [2 Timothy 4:1–2]

There is a great tendency in modern times to make the pulpit the place for the display of humor and wit. These please and draw but are not only foreign but antagonistic to the true ends of the ministry. Instead of giving vent to these sallies of trifling and humor, one ought to restrain them. Rowland Hill was a great wit and frequently gave way to his native impulse in the pulpit, but being so genuine a Christian he was filled with deep repentance for thus offending against the true interests of his Lord and of souls. After one of these bursts of humor, which excited laughter to a considerable degree in the congregation, he turned at once to repair the evil by an awful address to their consciences, breaking their hearts into tears. After Mr. Hill had retired for the night, the gentleman at whose house he was staying heard someone in the passage and found Mr. Hill at the foot of the stairs in deep agony of mind, unable to ascend to his room. Mr. Hill gave vent to his agony by confessing sorrow at having been such a trifler, and mourned with the simplicity of a child over his unseasonable drollery. Before he went to his room he said, "I never wish to say a single word, which would excite a smile, which would prevent an immediate approach to God in all the solemnity of spiritual prayer."

His friend and biographer says, "It almost always happened that whenever he had given way to his natural disposition for the ludicrous, or had been more than usually eccentric in his manner, there followed a lowness of spirits, and he then acknowledged the regret he felt at having been led away by any levity of mind while engaged in the solemn service of the pulpit." His agony and deep repentance on an occasion of this kind, says his biographer, "was most affecting, and was a striking proof of his contrition when he reflected that by giving way to the natural sprightliness of his disposition he might have prevented his real usefulness, or have forgotten for an instant the character of a messenger of the gospel."

Of Robert McCheyne his biographer says, "He wished to be always in the presence of God—a remarkably solemn ministry." The sainted Bishop Andrew said to us in regard to a preacher of splendid gifts: "No person would send for him on a dying bed; he laughs too much." Charles Simeon had Henry Martyn's picture over his fireplace and said of it: "No one looks at me as he does. He never takes his eyes off me! and seems always to be saying, 'Be serious, be in earnest—don't trifle, don't trifle!'" And the earnest, holy Simeon was always answering back: "I will be serious; I won't trifle, I won't trifle."

# 14

## Preaching That Kills
### *April 2, 1892*

BY a slight perversion, the sweetest graces may bear the bitterest fruit. The sun gives life, but sunstrokes are death. Preaching is to give life. It may also kill. The preacher holds the keys; he may lock as well as unlock. Preaching is God's great institution for the planting and maturing of spiritual life. When properly executed its benefits are untold; when wrongly executed no evil can exceed its damaging results. It is an easy matter to destroy the flock if the shepherd be unwary or the pasture be destroyed; easy to capture the citadel if the watchmen be asleep or the food and water be poisoned. Since preaching is invested with such gracious prerogatives, exposed to so great evils, involved with so many grave responsibilities, it would be a parody on the shrewdness of the devil, and a libel on his character and reputation, if he did not bring his master influences to adulterate the preacher and the preaching. In face of all this, the exclamatory interrogatory of Paul, "Who is sufficient for these things?" is never out of order.

Paul says: "Our sufficiency is of God; who also hath made us able ministers of the new testament; not of the letter, but of the spirit; for the letter killeth, but the spirit giveth life" (2 Cor. 3:5–6). The true ministry is God-touched, God-enabled, and God-made. The Spirit of God is on the preacher in anointing power and the fruit of the Spirit is in his heart. The Spirit of God has vitalized the man and the word. His preaching gives life, gives life as the spring gives life, gives life as the resurrection gives life, gives ardent life as the summer gives ardent life, gives fruitful life as the autumn gives fruitful life. The life-giving preacher is a man whose heart is ever athirst for God, whose soul is ever following hard after God, whose eye is single to God, and in whom, by the power of God's Spirit, the flesh and the world have been crucified. The ministry of this preacher is like the generous flood of a life-giving river.

The preaching that kills is nonspiritual preaching. The ability of the preaching is not from God. Lower sources than God have given to it energy and stimulant. The Spirit is not evident in the preacher nor in his preaching. Many kinds of forces may be projected and stimulated by preaching that kills, but they are not spiritual forces. They may resemble spiritual forces, but they are only shadow, counterfeit; they may seem to have life, but the life is not real. The preaching that kills is the letter; shapely and orderly it may be, but it is the letter still, the dry, husky letter, the empty, bald shell. The letter may have the germ of life in it, but it has no breath of spring to evoke it; winter seed it is, as hard as the winter's soil, as icy as the winter's air. No thawing will take place and no germination. This letter preaching has the truth; but even divine truth has no life-giving energy alone, it must be energized by the Spirit, with all God's forces at its back. "Truth unquickened" by God's Spirit deadens as much, or more, than error. It may be pure truth, but without the Spirit its shade and touch are deadly. The letter preaching is unctionless, neither mellowed nor oiled by the Spirit. There may be tears, but tears cannot run God's machinery; tears may be but summer's breath on a snow-covered iceberg, nothing but surface slush. Feelings and earnestness there may be, but it is the emotion of the actor and the earnestness of the attorney. The preacher may feel the kindling of his own sparks, be eloquent over his own exegesis, and be earnest in delivering the product of his own brain. The professor may usurp the place and imitate the fire of the apostle—brains and nerves may serve the place and feign the work of God's Spirit—and by these forces the letter may glow and sparkle like an illumined text, but the glow and sparkle will be as barren of life as the field sown with pearls.

The preaching that kills may be, and generally is, orthodox, dogmatically, inviolably orthodox. We love orthodoxy. It is good. It is the best. It is the clean, clear-cut teaching of God's Word. Orthodoxy is the trophies won by truth in its conflict with error, the levees that faith has raised against the desolating floods of honest or reckless misbelief or unbelief; but orthodoxy, clear and hard as crystal, suspicious and militant, may be but the letter well shaped, well named, and well learned, the letter that kills. Nothing is so dead as a dead orthodoxy, too dead to speculate, too dead to think, to study, or to pray.

The preaching that kills may have insight and grasp of principles, may be scholarly and critical in taste, may exhibit knowledge of all the minutiae concerning the derivation and grammar of the letter, may be able to trim the letter into its perfect pattern and illumine it as Plato and Cicero may be illumined, may study it as a lawyer studies his textbooks to form his brief or defend his case, and yet be like a frost, a killing frost. Letter preaching may be eloquent, enameled with poetry and rhetoric, sprinkled with prayer, spiced with sensation, illumined by genius, and yet be a corpse in a massive, chaste coffin with costly mountings, surrounded by rare and beautiful flowers. The preaching that kills may be without scholarship, unmarked by any freshness of thought or feeling, clothed in tasteless generalities or vapid specialties, with sloven, irregular style and may reflect neither closet nor study, and not be graced by thought, expression, or prayer. Under such preaching how wide and utter the desolation! how profound the spiritual death!

This letter preaching deals with the surface and shadow of things, and not with the things themselves. It does not penetrate the inner part. It has no deep insight into, no strong grasp of, the hidden life of God's Word. It is true to the outside, but the outside is the hull, which must be broken and penetrated for the kernel. The letter may be dressed so as to attract and be fashionable, but the attraction is not toward God, nor is the fashion for heaven. The failure is in the preacher. God has not made him. He has never been in the hands of God like clay in the hands of the potter. He has been busy about the sermon, its thought and finish, its drawing and impressive forces; but the deep things of God have never been sought, studied, fathomed, or experienced by him. He has never stood before "the throne high and lifted up," never heard the seraphim song, never seen the vision, nor felt the rush of that awful holiness and cried out in utter abandon and despair under the sense of weakness and guilt. He has never had his life renewed, his heart touched, purged, and inflamed by the live coal from God's altar. His ministry may draw people to him, to the church, and to the form and ceremony, but it won't truly draw people to God, to sweet, holy, divine communion with him. By this letter preaching the church has been patched up but not edified, pleased but not sanctified. Life is suppressed, a chill is in the summer air, the soil is baked and hard. The city of our God becomes the city of the dead. The church is a graveyard, not an embattled army. Praise and prayer are stifled and worship is dead. The preacher and the preaching have helped sin, not holiness and have peopled hell, not heaven.

# 15

## Conditions of Growth
### *April 28, 1892*

It is a matter of universal agreement that religion is a thing of growth. Advancement is not only a condition of its prosperity but of its life. It has been received as an axiom that there is no standing still in religion. This is the theory, but in the realm of practice there is nothing in which there is so much standing still as in religion. There are few things like religion that have such capacities and possibilities for growth and agencies to secure growth, but in which there is so little growing. Peter, in one comprehensive statement, gives some of the necessary conditions of growth. "Wherefore," he says, "laying aside all malice, and all guile, and hypocrisies, and envies, and all evil speakings. As newborn babes, desire the sincere milk of the word, that ye may grow thereby" (1 Peter 2:1–2).

Life is the basis of growth. The newborn babe, helpless and inactive though it be, grows because it is a living thing. Dead substances do not grow. In our spirits there must be the implantation of spiritual life as the germinal basis of growth. Spiritual birth and babyhood must precede spiritual manhood. We grow in grace and in the knowledge of the Lord Jesus Christ. We grow up into Christ in all things. We grow in spiritual beauty "as the lily." We grow in spiritual fruitfulness "as the vine." We grow in strength "as the cedar of Lebanon." We grow in holiness "as a temple of the Lord."

There are hindrances to the spiritual life that not only retard its growth but constantly menace it. These hindrances are in the heart—in the hearts of God's regenerate ones—and are to be laid aside, not so easily, but as really and as fully as we lay aside our garments for our beds, or our bodies in death. The first in order, if not in degree of these hindrances is malice, which is a feeling of evil in the heart against someone with or without cause. Religion is to love enemies as well as friends; it can neither thrive nor exist in a soil of ill or embittered feelings. The cherishing of, or even allowing, the feeling of malice against anyone arrests all spiritual growth. Malice, like salt, curses with spiritual barrenness the soil where it is found. Like a midsummer freeze it is death to the most luxuriant growth. As the presence of the smallest atom of leaven vitiated the Passover, so the presence of malignity in its mildest form depraves spiritual life and impedes its growth. As the Jew searched with lighted candle every nook and corner and crevice that he might cast out all hidden leaven as a preparation for the Passover, so all malice against anyone must be searched and cast out.

Guile is the second hindrance to order, which is to be gotten rid of. Guile is insincerity, the speaking by act or lip what the heart does not say. Guile is doubleness—a double face that looks two ways, double lips that speak two ways, a double heart that feels two ways. Guile throws out the bait by which we expect to catch people. It is neither real nor sincere. It is only to attract people, using the bait of flattery to draw them toward us. Religion cannot grow in the soil of insincerity. Hollowness or deceit are as foreign to it as heaven is to hell. Sincerity is the pure honey of religion. One of the essential characteristics of a true Israelite is that he be without guile. Insincerity is one of the native, radical, and gigantic evils of the heart. It must be rooted out or religion dies.

Hypocrisy means acting a part or veiling the heart so that one's true feelings cannot be seen. Judas was a hypocrite because he was no real apostle, only acting the part of one. Acting a part in worship is hypocrisy. We may say with the lips that which is not in the heart; the lips in prayer and praise, but the heart silent or far away. All acting a part must be put away. The heart must be full, and the lips the true channel of the heart. Religion cannot feed on make-believes, pretenses, or professions. Shams must be renounced; all must be true in religion. It cannot be carried on by actors. Mere performances kill religion; they create a frigid zone in which all religion freezes stone dead.

Envy seems to be a little thing, a burst of passion or an uneasy, painful sensation at the good of others, but it must go or religion goes. Envy sold Joseph into Egypt, delivered Christ into the hands of Pilate, and is the author of a world of mischief. Envy is the child of ambition and bears the depraved likeness of its depraved father. It hates the successful, because of their successes. It hates the good because of their goodness. It violates love and stands midway in the fearful catalogue of the works of the flesh; murder and drunkenness follow in its train. It is a petty, mean, little fire that kindles great things.

All evil speakings, says the apostle, must be put off. The heart must be cleansed and the tongue silenced from evil. The fountain must be cleansed, and the stream kept pure. Digging out these noxious weeds, curing these inbred heart-sins, putting off these defiled garments that we got from our father Adam, the heirloom of his sin and of our shame, requires patient, radical dealing, but when we get rid of them we will be able to grow, which is the point that the apostle makes. Dr. Clarke states the case strongly and well. He says: "It is when the soul is purified from all sin that it can properly grow in grace and in the knowledge of our Lord Jesus Christ; as the field may be expected to produce a good crop and all the seed vegetate when the thorns, thistles, briers, and noxious weeds of every kind are grubbed out." How can the divine seed grow when the soil is exhausted and the life poisoned by the shade and presence of these weeds of sin? If exercise and effort are conducive to growth, then the spiritual vigor, exercise, and fruits of faith involved in getting rid of "all malice, and all guile, and hypocrisies, and envies, and all evil speakings" will give abundant growth and spiritual health.

A vigorous appetite for spiritual food is an important condition of growth. A strong desire for the sincere milk of the Word lies at the base of all spiritual growth. The appetite must be cured of all depraved tastes and healthy tastes must be cultivated.

The spiritual taste is corrupted by sin just as our tongues can be dulled by unwholesome or highly spiced food. Homely, plain meals are good remedies for weakened appetites and good appetizers for our palates. The appetite that is satisfied by spiritual growth must be strong in character and healthy in tone. It must clamor like the babe for its own pure food and have no tolerance for anything else. It must demand pastors who, with the tender solicitude and yearning of a mother will give the God-appointed food, the sincere milk of the Word. Food, pure food, is the essential of growth. The food that makes religion grow is the preached Word of God. The Word of God is taken into the life of the preacher as his food and given out as the mother gives our her own life to nourish her babe. No mixing is desired, no spice added to the food, no water added to the milk. The pure Word is what nourishes the soul, not speeches about the Word, nor the philosophy of the Word, but the Word itself. The hungry man is not fed by discourses about the uses or the necessity of bread, nor about the philosophy of its elements, nor the process of its making. Only give the bread to him and his digestive and assimilative functions will take care of the analysis and distribution. Nothing feeds the spiritual nature as well as good preaching. The pure word of God preached by God's commissioned and anointed servant rectifies, invigorates, and develops the whole spiritual constitution. Bad preaching is a great corrupter of piety. The preacher who gratifies itching ears not only deadens the ear and turns the heart away from the truth but "turns it unto fables."

The soul that truly seeks God to the uprooting of these inbred constitutional defects, whose appetite hungers after the pure food of the soul, and who gets that food dispensed with a wise and liberal hand from God's supply "will grow thereby unto salvation."

# 16

## Ambition Hinders Preaching
### *May 19, 1892*

AMBITION is one of the greatest hindrances to preaching. Ambition is born of self and nurtured by pride. It manifests itself in various ways: the desire to be a great preacher, to have the first place, to be a leader, or to secure places of honor or profit. It veils itself under many disguises. It is christened with the surname "laudable," and by that baptismal name it comes into the church and works out its selfish, worldly schemes. A person may be a Christian by name and be a church member, but if he is driven by ambition, he is an infidel at heart and of the world worldly. The days of the prevalence of ambition in the church have been the days of supreme church worldliness and extreme apostasy.

There is much in a name, and the prudent Christian will not allow this corrupter of the faith to enter, though clothed in an ever-so-pleasing garb of innocent names. Christian faith has kindled and consecrated the flame of holy zeal, stimulating and giving ardor to effort. True zeal is a heavenly fire, the purity of which disdains all earthly adulterations. Zeal crucifies self; zeal fixes its eyes on both God and his glory. As Christ died for sin once, so the Christian by crucifixion dies to self and says, not by rote or in the poetry of ecstatic feeling but truly,

"Perish every fond ambition." In every moment of his life, in every vision of his eye, in every impulse of his heart, in every effort of his hand, he is true to the fact as well as to the poetry of this self-renouncing commitment.

Ambition is the one thing that affected the power, the peace, and the piety of the apostles of our Lord. We see its effects noted in their envies and strife. A few instances are recorded. How much unrecorded jealousy and alienation was produced, we can only conjecture. We have the record of its existence and Christ's rebuke in the early part of their career and its violence breaks out under the shadow of the cross. The bitter thoughts of his death are mixed with the strife of his disciples for place and his solemn charge against the religious phase of worldly ambition. The washing of the disciples' feet was the last act of personal training that Christ used as the remedy for ambition in his disciples.

Ambition destroys the foundation of Christian character by making faith impossible. Faith roots itself in the soil where selfish and worldly growths have been destroyed. "How can ye believe," says Christ, "which receive honor one of another, and seek not the honor that cometh from God only?" (John 5:44). In this statement is shown the impossibility of blending faith with the desire to receive honor from men. The entrance of this alluring element of human honor draws the heart from the honor that comes from God and sweeps away the foundations of faith. When the eye seeks things other than God, when the heart desires things other than God—this is ambition. No man can serve these two masters; no man can combine the ends of self and of God. He may think he can; he may seem to do so; but no one can perform this spiritual impossibility.

Ambition enthrones pride, and that is the throne on which Satan sits. Humility is destroyed by ambition. The history of the church attests to the fact that humility has no place in the church that is ambitious nor in the religion of an ambitious ecclesiastic. Humility is not a virtue of those who have sought to be put in the calendar of earthly saints. No ambition is so proud as an ecclesiastical ambition, none less scrupulous. No church can be more thoroughly apostate than the church whose leaders have come into their places through the secret or open byways of ambition. No ambition is so destructive as that, which comes in under the guise of religion. Ambition is worldly, though it may be disguised under the name of religion. It easily deludes its possessor, under the plea of a wider field of influence and usefulness; but the presence of ambition, like the soil of Sardinia, embitters even the honey.

If ambition can be religious and can preach, it must do so without love; for love and ambition can no more unite than can light and darkness; they are as essentially at war as Christ and Belial. "Love seeketh not her own," while ambition is ever seeking its own, and not infrequently it seeks with all its heart that which is another's. Love in honor prefers one another; this ambition never does.

If Jesus Christ is to be our model preacher; if our attachment to him rises to anything above an impure sentiment, then the mind that was in him must be in us. He was without taint of ambition. In the revised version we have this attitude of Christ to ambition:

> Have this mind in you, which was also in Christ Jesus: who, being in the form of God counted it not a prize to be on an equality with God, but emptied himself, taking the form of a servant, being made in the likeness of men; and being found in fashion as a man, he humbled himself, becoming obedient even unto death, yea, the death of the cross.
>
> [Phil. 2:5–8]

The whole history and character of Christ are in direct antagonism to ambition.

If Paul is to serve as an example for preachers, it is at the point of freedom from all forms of ambition that his example is the most emphatic. He puts the whole inventory of ecclesiastical and earthly goods in one catalogue and renounces them all in this strong language: "But what things were gain to me,

those I counted loss for Christ. Yea doubtless, and I count all
things but loss for the excellency of the knowledge of Christ
Jesus my Lord: for whom I have suffered the loss of all things,
and do count them but dung, that I may win Christ" (Phil.
3:7–8); and as though this were not enough, he takes us to the
cross, where every earthly thing perished in pain, shame, and
utter bankruptcy, and declares; "I am crucified with Christ."

We have been unaware as many things have been allowed
to come into our religion and into our ministry and to defame
them, but nothing is more deadly to our religion than ambition.
It has in its bad embrace the seeds of all evil. It has insincerity
and hypocrisy. It is a sycophant, and a tyrant, a trimmer, and
a caterer. Of all the evils that grieve God's Spirit and quench
his flame, ambition may be reckoned among the chief, if not
the very chief. The fact that ecclesiastical pride, church sentiment, and church worldliness will allow ambition to be christened at church altars and have the stamp of innocence, and
even of virtue, on it is suggestive and ought to be alarming.

Is the desire for ecclesiastical advancement ambition? If not,
what is it? We may say it is a laudable ambition! Can a qualifying word change the evil nature of this dark and fallen angel?
Does an angelic garb make Satan an angel? We may say we want
a more honorable place to do more honorable and larger service
for Christ. Is not this Satan clothing himself as an angel of
good? The honor of a service done for God is in no way dependent on its honorable nature or largeness. The honor of service
for God depends only on the spirit in which it is done, and
that spirit is one in which self-pride and ambition are crucified.
Self in us looks to the future to largeness and honor. Christ in
us looks to the present to fidelity and zeal for the work at hand
and has no eye for self and the future.

Can the preacher preach without faith? He must do so if he
preaches with ambition, for in Christ's system faith and ambition cannot coexist. Can the preacher preach without love? If
he preaches with ambition he must, for ambition and love have
neither union nor concord. Can a preacher preach without

humility? If he preaches with ambition he must, for ambition is the very quintessence of pride. Can a worldly preacher preach? If he preaches with ambition he must, for ambition is worldliness in the concrete. Can a preacher preach without consecration? If he preaches with ambition he must, for ambition is a thing to be crucified, and not consecrated. Crucified, ambition must be; consecrated, it never can be.

Ambition changes the whole nature of ministry and floods it with worldliness. Instead of the ministry being an institution where the highest Christian graces are to be produced and the loftiest virtues exhibited, ambition transforms it into a ministry where self is the mainspring and every grace is blighted.

With ambition the church is no longer an institution to save men, where the preacher, like Christ, exhausts himself to secure this end; but it is changed into an institution to confer position on men, and all its holy places are polluted by the grasping, selfish hand of ambition or they are trodden by its unhallowed feet.

# 17

## Preparation to Hear
### *July 14, 1892*

WITHOUT preparation the preacher cannot preach to profit. Without preparation the hearer cannot hear to profit. Lack of preparation brings to naught many a preaching effort; failure to prepare brings spiritual leanness to many a hearer. The sermon may fail because the preacher has failed in prayerful and thoughtful preparation; the sermon may fail because of the want of thorough preparation in the pew. If the preacher can be charged as guilty who neglects preparation to preach, the hearer is exposed to the same charge who fails to make prayerful preparation to hear. It is to be feared that the pew is more negligent in the important duty of preparation than the pulpit. The loose, thoughtless, prayerless pulpit will soon be exposed and realize the embarrassment, if not the shame, of its failure; but the pew is exposed to no punishment of this kind, and can sin habitually without the fear of public exposure.

The serious consideration of the importance of preaching is the base motive for preparation. Preaching is a solemn matter not only for the preacher but for the hearer. To the hearer it is the Word of God, the instituted means of his salvation, the origin and culture of his faith, the quickener to every holy exercise and to every duty; it is the agent by which religion is built up in solidity, symmetry, and beauty. To hear the word of God is no small matter; it is our life; it is as milk to the babe, our God-appointed food by which we are nourished and made fat and flourishing in our religion. It is not a lecture, an entertainment, the whiling away an hour; but it is the incorruptible Word of God that liveth and abideth forever. The soil that receives this precious seed must be well prepared. Beaten oil for the sanctuary was the Lord's demand of those who served in the temple; beaten hearts prepared and compounded with care is his demand of those who wait in his sanctuary.

Closet prayer is one of the means of preparation. No Christian ought to think of going to the house of God who has not prepared his heart by a private approach to God. God's hand on the heart of the hearer in answer to prayer is the only true response to God's hand on the preacher. Prayer for God's help, for a collected and concentrated mind, for a devout and sincere heart, and for God's help to the preacher puts the soul in the divinest harmony with the occasion and secures its richest benefits.

The written Word of God devoutly read is a fitting preface to the hour for preaching. Bible lessons stored in the heart afford the best preparation for the teaching of the sermon. God's Word written should lay the foundation in the heart for God's Word preached. Meditation on that word and on God is a most happy preparation for hearing thoughtfully, prayerfully, and to edification God's preached word. Meditation is a most difficult but most valuable duty. It is difficult amid the noise, excitement, diversion, and surface nature of things; but it is valuable to quiet and fix the mind and to give depth and intensity to devotion. This sweet, comforting, elevating exercise best prepares the heart to enter God's house and to experience the nearest approach to and the fullest revelation of God.

The spirit with which we go to church and the motives that move us thither, all bring us into harmony or into discord with the solemn duties of this solemn hour. The thought of waiting on God, of meeting him, should possess us. We should not come as spectators. We should go far beyond the spirit of listeners, though our listening should be respectful and most attentive.

The preparation for hearing creates the right spirit for worshipers, filling their hearts with devotion, reverence, praise, and prayer and making them ready to receive God's Word. The receptive elements of worship—docility, meekness, and patience—make good soil in which the seed of God's Word can grow. The laying "apart all filthiness and superfluity of naughtiness" is as absolutely necessary to the preparation of the soil of the heart as the grubbing of the roots and stumps and the digging out of the weeds are to the natural soil and its crop.

To this preparation must be added longing for God and his house and an eager desire that puts gladness into our hearts when the hour comes for God's service. Like pious David, our soul will be reduced to one passionate plea: "That I may dwell in the house of the Lord all the days of my life, to behold the beauty of the Lord, and to inquire in his temple." If we combine with these the memory of God's goodness and mercy that awakens the deepest sense of gratitude and binds us stronger than a sweet and solemn oath to dwell in his house forever, then the preaching will not be a dull service, a mere entertainment, an intellectual or a sensuous feast, but it will be a feast to the soul, an hour of divine communion, of uplifting of heart and life, of forgetfulness of the world and divorce from it.

Preparation to hear is connected to a specific occasion. The time immediately preceding and during the service has weighty and special demands for readiness and reception, but the preparation to hear does not begin nor end with the special service. It should be as extensive as the life, involving the life, the character, all habits, and the everyday devotional spirit. This preparation is not part of the public worship but bears in a direct and most potent way on the special seasons of public worship.

Well did Christ say, "Take heed therefore how ye hear." We need the grace and the caution of hearing. The grace of hearing in the pew will add much to the grace of speaking in the pulpit. Anointed ears are as essential as anointed tongues. We should cry for the baptism of the Spirit for hearing as well as for the baptism of the Spirit for speaking.

# 18

# Simplicity in Preaching
## *August 31, 1892*

MR. Wesley says in the preface to his sermons:

Nothing here appears in an elaborate, elegant, or oratorical dress. I design plain truth for plain people; therefore of set purpose I abstain from all nice and philosophical speculations; from all perplexed and intricate reasonings, and as far as possible from even the show of learning, unless in sometimes citing the original scripture. I labor to avoid all words not easy to be understood, all which are not used in common life; and in particular those kind of technical terms that so frequently occur in books of divinity, those modes of speaking, which men of reading are intimately acquainted with, but which to common people are an unknown tongue. My decision is in some sense to forget all that ever I have read in my life. I mean to speak in the general as if I had never read one author, ancient or modern (always excepting the inspired). I am persuaded that, on the one hand, this may be a means of enabling me more clearly to express the sentiments of my heart, while I simply follow the chain of my own thoughts without entangling myself with those of other men; and that on the other, I shall come with fewer weights upon my mind, with less of prejudice and prepossession either to search for myself or to deliver to others the naked truths of the gospel.

We believe that there is much wisdom in this method of
Wesley, that is, if one seeks only the glory of God in preaching.
Wesley had much study to secure this end, but he devoted himself to it with characteristic conscientiousness and perseverance. At the beginning of his ministry, he delivered a highly
finished sermon to a country congregation. They listened with
open mouths. He saw they did not understand what he said.
He struck out some of the hard sentences and tried it again.
Their mouths were only half open. He read the sermon to an
intelligent servant, asking her to point out the parts she did
not understand. She stopped him so often that he grew impa-
tient but persevered, writing a plain word for each hard one.
This method reduced his sermon to such simplicity that his
congregation understood every word. This process would save
many a sermon, which is otherwise wholly lost for any practical, edifying use.

President Finney, in his memoirs, writes that a friend of his
had to leave his church on account of ill health. He employed
a young man fresh from the seminary to supply his pulpit. This
young man wrote and preached as splendid sermons as he
could. The pastor's wife finally ventured to say to him, "You
are preaching over the heads of our people. They do not understand your language or illustrations." He replied, "I am a young
man; I am cultivating a style. I am aiming to prepare myself
for occupying a pulpit and surrounding myself with a cultivated congregation. I cannot descend to your people. I must
cultivate an elevated style."

President Finney kept his eye on the young man but never
found him connected with any revival of God's work amidst
all the great revivals that for many years blessed those regions.
God honors singleness of eye. The building up of a reputation
is duplicity; the looking after a reputation already gained is a
double dealing that God cannot and will not honor.

An old writer says, "The preacher should see only three
objects, namely, one God and two souls. The souls are his own
and his hearer's. For his fidelity to each of those who attend

his ministrations he must give account to God." The preacher who thus looks to God and souls makes preaching too serious a business to think of style, reputation, or self in any of its thousand forms. He will be too much in earnest for anything but the directness of a simplicity that has crucified self.

# 19

## The Secret
### *September 15, 1892*

WE may search out and account for the failure to preach
with profit in many ways, but the true secret of failure will be
found in the lack of urgent prayer in seeking God's presence
and power to qualify us to secure the spiritual results of the
occasion. Mr. Spurgeon is represented to have preached on
one occasion with great power and effect. The secret of the
spiritual energy of that occasion is revealed by the statement
that Mr. Spurgeon went to the pulpit with his face bathed in
tears from a season of prevailing prayer. Another occasion of
his preaching illustrates the true source of this great man's
great power and also the source of his failures. The circumstances are thus related:

A friend who knew him many years ago, and who heard him preach
on many occasions, says that he once heard him preach in an English
town in the afternoon and evening on a certain day, and that at the
close of the afternoon service, Mr. Spurgeon spoke of the consciousness that the service had not been what it should have been. His
friend (then a student) admitted that he thought the preacher had
not been himself in the preaching. Mr. Spurgeon, with a remark to
the effect that it would never do to repeat the failure in the evening,
went out into the woods to pray. Indeed, he spent the whole interval

between the afternoon and evening services in prayer. The latter
meeting was one of great power and different in all respects from
that of the afternoon.

This case is a representative one. There is no royal road to
preaching. The way of humility and prayer, the constant depen-
dence on the Holy Ghost, the constant and importunate seeking of the Holy Ghost by a faith and prayer that recognize the
absolute helplessness of other agencies to give efficiency to the
service, and a mighty travail of spirit that God's efficiency would
be bestowed—this only can secure for preaching spiritual efficacy and results.

There are men who can write and read, or deliver without
writing, masterly sermons, masterly as cultured or intellectual
productions, which may make an impression after their order;
but the masterly production is not after God's order, neither
is the impression for God's glory. The men who, by their preaching, mightily influence their congregations for God are the men
who come from the closet, where their faith and prayer have
prevailed with and conquered God, to the pulpit, where they
prevail with and conquer men for God. All things being equal,
or being unequal, the preachers who are the mightiest in the
pulpit with men for God are the ones who are the mightiest
in their closets with God for men.

# 20

# Led by the Spirit
## *October 6, 1892*

To be led by the Spirit of God is a very gracious and high state. Doubtless, many mistake their own suggestions for the suggestions of God's Spirit. But notwithstanding the fact that errors and fanaticism exist in regard to the doctrine of being led by the Spirit, it is a spiritual reality that we can be led by the Spirit, familiar and responsive to his slightest touch and hearing and obeying his gentlest whisper. To those who have surrendered to the Spirit's direction, who seek his guidance and yield implicitly to it, his voice and his touch are familiar.

Mr. Spurgeon was a very spiritual man. He was a master builder, proficient in spiritual things, and his example deserves thoughtful consideration. We should be challenged to examine, if not imitate, any point he makes in regard to spiritual operations.

In one point he differed from many popular preachers. Dr. Pierson discusses this point:

> Mr. Spurgeon did not like to preannounce a special sermon for a particular date or indicate the subjects on which he intended to preach, for he said to himself, "How can I tell what I may be led at the time to feel is the will of God, or what new communications it may please God to make to me, which may demand a revolution to my plans."

He would never predict what his utterance was to be, for just before he went into the pulpit, or even after it, the sermon might take a new shape, or might even shape itself upon a new theme.

It has never been to our taste, this preannouncement of themes. There is something that does not commend itself to us as the thing to do. That there should be the most prayerful and thoughtful study preceding the sermon, as opportunity allows, is among first principles. That the Spirit does not suggest to or lead a lazy man or a trifler is clear, but the most careful preparation should not shut the door to the freedom of spiritual direction. We believe that many preachers are divested of all spiritual force in their preaching because they are spiritual loungers or slovens. On the other hand, we believe a greater number of preachers shut out the aid of the Holy Spirit by the rigid stereotyped preparations they make, leaving no room for the Spirit to impress and enlarge or direct. The Holy Ghost must have freedom, or he will have nothing. Dr. Pierson, in his agreement with Mr. Spurgeon in his opposition to the pre-announcement of preaching subjects, says:

We contend most earnestly that this is the only frame of mind for any one who speaks as one that declares the oracles of God—he must hold himself open to the latest impressions of the oracle-breathing Spirit. Preoccupation of mind, like the preoccupation of the inn at Bethlehem, may either keep out the Lord, or drive him, as it were, into a corner.

# 21

## Personal Preaching
### *October 13, 1892*

DEAL with the sin and not with the sinner is a maxim of popular acceptance, but like most popular maxims when adopted by the pulpit it makes sad havoc of truth and righteousness. The sin and the sinner are inseparable. Sin is not an abstract entity. It has its being through the sinner. Sin is not an accountable thing. The sinner is accountable for the sin. The only way to destroy the sin is through the sinner. We reach the sin when we reach the sinner. Our gospel is a personal gospel. "Thou art the man" is the epitome of its purpose. To separate and purge the person from his sins is the chief aim of the gospel.

An impersonal ministry will never save, for under such a ministry sin will thrive with its rankest and most poisonous growth. A personal ministry is not simply for the impenitent, but it has its mission to the church and to the best in the church. The presence of sin in church members stays their advance in holiness and scatters or dims the light they ought to shed on the regions around.

This is the rub: men do not like personal preaching as a rule. Such a ministry often disturbs and annoys. It collides with one's desires, gratification, or interest. A personal ministry is often

felt as an intruder on privileged ground; the rebukes are
received as scoldings. They become intolerable by repetition.
The chief function of the ministry is personal. Its mission
is to the man. Its design is to present every man perfect. Mr.
Gladstone has spoken some words on this point. They are wise
words and much to our mind. He says:

One thing I have against the clergy, both in country and in the towns.
I do not know whether the reproach applies to ministers of other congregations. I think they are not severe enough on their congregations.
They do not sufficiently lay upon the souls and consciences of their
hearers their moral obligations and probe their hearts and bring up
their whole lives and action to the bar of conscience. The class of
sermons which, I think are most needed, are of the class, one of which
so offended Lord Melbourne long ago. Lord Melbourne was one day
seen coming from church in the country in a mighty fume. Finding
a friend, he exclaimed, "It is too bad. I have always been a supporter
of the church, and I have always upheld the clergy. But it is really too
bad to have to listen to a sermon like that we have had this morning.
Why! the preacher actually insisted upon applying religion to a man's
private life!" But that is the kind of preaching which I like best—the
kind of preaching which men need most, but it is also the kind which
they get least. The clergy are afraid of dealing faithfully with their
hearers. And I fear, although I have not the same data for forming
an opinion, that this is equally true of the Nonconformist ministers.
Mr. Spurgeon, I admit, was not so. He was a good and brave man,
and my remark does not apply to him. But there is not enough of
such searching preaching in any of our pulpits.

We would think that the clergy of the established Church
of England would be entirely free from this fault, having their
livings secure, raised as they are above the clamor of popular
opposition, independent as to salary and position. To deal in
vague or splendid generalities, to deal with impersonal subjects
or faraway sins seems to be the faulty and almost universal tendency of the pulpit. The modern pulpit is much intent on being
a popular pulpit. It has the praiseworthy end of getting the
people to church but the serious defect of impersonality. The
itching after popularity means that the pulpit cannot be plain,

wholly honest, or personal in its rebukes. Popularity must be tolerant, apologetic, and impersonal in its censures. Personal preachers are the ones that reach hearts and consciences. They make men feel their sins. They expose the sin till the sinner realizes that the sin is part of himself, that its enormity and guilt are his, that its shame and punishment belong to him. The personal preacher does not preach to the times, but to the men who make the times and are responsible for the times.

The old preachers had at the close of their sermon what they called the application. All the vagaries and intellectual or other wanderings ended up at the person. He was made to feel, however wide and discursive the main part had been, that the hunt was for him. It is better to fire the last shot at the man, though the others were all wasted, than not to fire at him at all.

A personal ministry takes its stand on that immutable principle of the gospel that personal purity is God's great aim and that this aim cannot be secured but by a personal ministry. Men are trying to get to heaven by proxy. They are proposing all kinds of substitutes for this personal purity. The church is substituting for this purity ritualism and gorgeous ceremony in some of its branches. Other churches are accepting in the stead of this personal purity the activity and busy churchly or organized doings of their members. Large gifts of money cover, and, in a measure in ecclesiastical circles, atone for the lack of this personal purity. So the popular trend is to do away with the purity or holiness of the individual as a prime factor in the life of the church. In such a church a personal ministry becomes offensively unpopular, and an impersonal ministry catches the popular breezes and currents. Charles the First said: "I carry my ears to hear other preachers, but I carry my conscience to hear Bishop Sanderson." Men carry their ears to an impersonal pulpit, and itching ears make infidel hearts. There are not too many pulpits to which men carry their consciences. An impersonal pulpit will neither make nor guide consciences. The nation and the church need pulpits that will make consciences for men who have none, consciences formed after God's Word.

A personal pulpit is the only sin-convicting pulpit. A personal pulpit is the only sin-destroying pulpit. A personal pulpit is the only edifying pulpit. Holiness can only be advanced by a personal pulpit. Holiness and all its attendant graces are blasted and die under an impersonal pulpit.

Personal preaching does not mean to call names, to be bad tempered, or to set the pulpit at war with the pew. It means to so classify and individualize the sermon so that its whole force centers on each individual, and no one is able to lose himself in the crowd. Impersonal preaching is to entertain or please. It may charm and bind with its spell, but it is only a picture, and that not of the man. Personal preaching is like a faithful mirror that puts the man with all his sins and weaknesses before his own eyes. Preaching ought to individualize, search, and uncover us, as the great day of judgment will individualize, search, and uncover us. Surface preaching, dealing with the veneer of human nature, will not do that. Personal preaching, like the chastening of God, for the present is not joyous, but grievous; nevertheless, afterward it will yield the peaceable fruits of righteousness to them who are exercised thereby. Personal preaching accounts for the stir in some churches. After the long night and death of impersonal preaching, the resurrection stir and day of personal preaching begins when spiritual matters are lively and painful. If the process of life is allowed to go on, and the personal preacher not voted a troubler of Israel, gracious results will follow. An impersonal ministry pleases, makes a reputation, and is popular. A personal ministry advances religion, saves sinners, perfects saints, and fills heaven.

# 22

## The Preacher Prepared
### *November 24, 1892*

REVIVALS are not simply devices to recover a backslidden church, nor are they only methods to repair spiritual waste. The revival is not emotional where the feelings are indulged in an excited religious way. A revival is not a thaw to be followed by a hardier freeze. A revival is God's coming to his church to give it aggressive power and lead it to victory. Such a visitation by God will heal backslidings, will arrest and restore spiritual waste, will draw the heart to the mightiest interests, will thaw the ice, will sub-soil the hardest ground; but beside these the revival will implant profound principles in the plowed soil and will penetrate by its divine life the heart riven by the excitement and convictions of the hour. Revivals have in them the force of a revolution. The revival can be like a pent-up earthquake that lets loose its spiritual energies while breaking through the surface hardened by worldliness and sin. The revival is not an expedient, an afterthought, an irregular or abnormal proceeding induced by the desperation of the case or made necessary by the failure of the regular and proper means. Revivals are numbered in the charter rights of the church. They belong to Methodists by a diviner right. They are theirs by birthright—an inalienable right save by their criminal forfeiture. Methodism can no more dispense with the revival and remain Methodist than it can surrender its life. Revivals to Methodism are the arteries that supply her heart, and fill all her veins. To secure a deep, thorough, pervasive revival ought to be of the first concern to every Methodist pastor and to every Methodist church. The revival must not be made the substitute when the pastor or church has failed or neglected the people. It must not be stressed so that it may manufacture spiritual reputation or swell the roll for Conference reports. Revival should be sought as an enduring force, as a mighty spiritual event, as the only remedy for the giant and prevalent ills that afflict the world.

To begin the revival in the right way and at the right place is of first importance. The preacher is an important factor in the revival. To insure the best results, the best in power and permanency, the revival must begin in him, continue in him, and in him produce its richest fruit. The revival ought to bear the preacher on its wave of highest advance. He must feel the keenest pangs of its birth. He should drink the gall of its bitterest beginnings. He should be clothed with the garb of its deepest humility. His tears should make its valley of Baca a well. The preacher who has not the power of faith to beget the revival, and who is not familiar with the regions marked by its highest wave will not be able to garner its fruits and preserve them as enduring spiritual supplies, and as the basis of future progress. The preacher ought to get more of spiritual good out of his revival than any one else. Its storm center of sublime power ought to be in him. He ought to have his hand on the valve and his feet on the wheel. He ought to be as familiar with all the bearings, bendings, outs, and ins of the revival as the best of pilots is with the river. He ought to know when the spirits are subject to the prophets and when they are running away with the prophets. God ought to be able to find in the pastor the place to begin his gracious work, as well as to find in the pastor a leader for the work; for the preacher who has not given his own heart to God for the place to begin this great work will never be God's anointed leader for the work.

The spiritual preparation of the preacher is the first step in the revival. This demand for a specific and more spiritual preparation, for a specific and mightier spiritual work, is no charge against the general fidelity of the preacher; but even here doubtless there would be found much cause for shame, humiliation, and confession but it is the Gethsemane preparation for the conflict and redemption of Calvary. It is the specific, careful, and heart-searching preparation for a great battle and a great victory. This preparation gauges our ability to go to the deepest depths and rise to the highest heights of spiritual success, and it gauges our ability to lead God's people to unparalleled successes.

The great hindrance to the work of the Lord in many places is found in the preacher himself. His orthodoxy may be faultless, his earnestness sincere, and his courage risen to the point of heroism, but somehow the man, the inner man, in its secret places, has never been broken down before God. His inner life has never been a great highway of holiness. Somehow self and not God has gotten into his holiest of holies. He stands dauntless before his people clothed with the ermine of righteousness and truth, but somehow and somewhere, all unconscious to himself, some spiritual nonconductor has touched his inner being, and the divine current has been arrested. His inner man has never felt its deep spiritual bankruptcy, its utter powerlessness. Self-esteem and ability, somehow, in the shape of literacy and proficiency in preaching have severed the delicate connection, or jostled the trolley off of the line. The experience of many pastors will attest the truth of these utterances. An illustration called the "Preacher Prepared" will suggest to many a faithful pastor the duty and the manner that preparation for revival should take. To go through the process this pastor did to secure his great revival is to be assured of results that will glorify God and work a mighty transformation in any church

and every community. This pastor, who was so deeply concerned for a revival, wrote,

> I had seen so many revivals averted by the condition of pastors, that
> I devoted the entire week of prayer to a preparation of my own heart
> and life. I believed that I was a Christian, but I wanted to see myself
> as God saw me. I wanted to be thoroughly humbled and completely
> emptied of self. I wanted to press upon the church and the world the
> overwhelming motives of God's eternal word with all the magnetism
> of a fervid, confident, loving, divine spirit. In pleading with Jehovah
> for others I would obey his command: "Be ye clean that bear the ves-
> sels of the Lord." On Monday I considered the infinitely holy character
> of God. By this stupendous theme my soul was greatly awed. On
> Tuesday I considered by own particular sins, in the presence of that
> Jehovah with whom even the solemn meeting may be iniquity. I asked
> myself, "What of your pride, ambition, self-seeking? What have you
> lacked in love, trust, spirituality, improvement of time, and toil for
> the lost?" On Wednesday I considered God's kindness to me, my fam-
> ily, and my church. I was amazed at his munificence. I was abashed
> at my own unthankfulness. But he has snatched away my loved ones,
> yet he enabled me to say: "O God, thy will be done; my Jesus, as thou
> wilt." On Thursday my questions were: "Why do you want a revival
> of religion? Is it chiefly to build up one man or one church, to make
> your people more genial and loving? Or, are you seeking, first of all,
> to honor Jesus in the salvation of the perishing? Have you been asking
> God for things which you do not expect to receive and which you
> make slight effort to secure?" By this time I was ready to cry with the
> apostle, "O wretched man that I am, who shall deliver me from the
> body of this death?" On Friday I was prepared as never before to look
> to Jesus. Mere earthly advantages seemed to me like the idle wind; I
> confessed and loathed my sin. I looked upon him whom I had pierced,
> and I mourned for him. I laid myself upon his altar, to do and to suffer
> his will. With great confidence I sought his Spirit. My view was def-
> inite; my feeling was deep: my soul was filled with confidence and
> peace. Each evening during the week I had poured forth to my church
> the experience of the day. At the close of the Friday meeting numbers
> exclaimed: "O what a meeting we have had!" The great revival had
> commenced.

A revival of this kind costs the preacher much, but it is cheap
at any price. There are revivals that cost the preacher nothing

but the money he raises to pay the helping brother. We need revivals that cost the pastor the death to self and the crucifixion to the world; revivals that are born in the travail of his own soul. We need revivals that will come to our Methodist preachers as the sun arose to Jacob in the fullness of its eastern splendor, the presage and symbol of victory after the long night of darkness, of struggle, of doubt, and of pain.

It is a law of spiritual generation that the converts take their spiritual shape and features from the condition of the church that begets them. If the church is cold and stiff the converts come in as newborn icicles, frozen at birth, or soon thereafter. If the church is fired with zeal, full of holiness, if it has an experience of what repentance, faith, and prayer are, then the converts are shaped by these principles. The revival that transmits these mighty spiritual forces to the generation coming on springs from the heart of a church, which is impregnated with these great truths. The revival that goes deep and stays long must come out of the heart of the church. As our Lord had a consuming desire to eat the Passover with his disciples, so must his church have a consuming desire to drink this new and richest wine of the kingdom and impart it to others.

The church must be in travail for souls as trophies to bring before the Lord, to give for the pledges of his favor. The church must bear on her heart the sin of others, its existence causing humiliation and sorrow. The church must draw nigh to God. "The sinners in Zion are afraid, fearfulness hath surprised the hypocrites." The hands of the church must be washed in innocency, and thus she must compass the altars of God, pleading for the revival. The extent of godlessness and impiety and God's impending vengeance should cause the church to cry out with the trembling prophet, "I have heard thy speech and was afraid: O Lord, revive thy work . . . in the midst of the years make known; in wrath remember mercy." The absence of song, the disappearance of joy should press the church to cry out: "Wilt thou not revive us again: that thy people may rejoice in thee?" All kinds of spiritual attitudes and all kinds of strong pleas should be in the mouth of the church and on her heart as evidence, not only of her willingness to receive the revival, but as indubitable proofs of her earnest longings for the coming of her Lord and the advancement of his work.

# Part Four

# 23

## Long or Short Sermons
### *March 2, 1893*

IN some quarters the demand is becoming clamorous for short sermons. A sermon of respectable length exhausts the patience and oppresses the nerves of the ordinary churchgoer, and the demand is made that the sermon be shortened to a length that the virile piety of the fathers would have deemed child's play. Spiritual quacks are prescribing short sermons as a remedy to relieve the invalid and oppressed pew. The short sermon is declared to be the cure for empty pews, but this remedy is a defective panacea. The short sermon will not cure but will rather establish the disease and make it chronic. The short sermon as a lure to attract men to church will not be worth its feathery weight. There will be nothing in it to attract and hold, for men are neither attracted nor held by empty nothings.

The cry for the short sermon springs from two sources. The first is the loss of spiritual nerve, taste, and stomach in the hearer. His spiritual appetite and digestion have been weakened or depraved, and a heavy, strong service is like a nightmare to him. The average hearer has no idea of the serious import of the occasion and is in haste to have it over, so if the sermon is weighty and moving, he may think that cutting it short and making it thin is the answer.

Another cause of this condition is the nature of the sermon. It is often but a mere human production, shorn of all the true elements of gospel preaching. It is professional, intellectual, without heart, a vain declamation, lacking many, if not all, of the essentials for proclaiming divine truth under the pressure of a divine hand that empowers, fills, and fires. Good gospel preaching will always have good gospel sense in it and will for God make the most out of the occasion and the conditions. Genuine preaching will tone up spiritual nerve, cultivate spiritual taste, and thicken spiritual blood so that a short sermon will be as objectionable as a scanty meal to a hungry man. This whole demand for short sermons can be hushed by pure gospel preaching. Earnestness and fidelity to God's Word and God's Spirit in the pulpit will beget prayer and a healthy appetite and digestion in the pew. Such a sermon will be a rich feast for which the taste is never satiated. Mr. Spurgeon's ministry was an illustration of this truth. Dr. Pierson, Mr. Spurgeon's successor, is a living case in point. The congregations, since his ministry began, have been larger than under Mr. Spurgeon's, and all the good results and incidental effects have improved rather than diminished under his ministry. This statement about his preaching makes the point:

Through all the oppressive heat of the past summer Dr. A. T. Pierson, who for eight months ministered with singular acceptance to Mr. Spurgeon's great congregation in London, has been preaching to full and often overflowing houses. The heat has often been extreme, the discourses have sometimes exceeded an hour, the services are plain to bareness, and preacher's manner, though earnest, is simple and quiet. There is, in fact, nothing to captivate the crowds that have thronged to hear him, except the one thing, a man of deep conviction and earnest purpose pleading with his fellowman to accept the life-giving truths of the gospel, to be reconciled to God through the crucified Saviour. That these truths, presented with "great plainness of speech," should have such attractive power at such a season, is a fresh and noteworthy demonstration of the power of preaching, when it is real preaching, of the kind of which Paul wrote. The preaching of Christ crucified has not lost its power. Men do not try to crowd that out of the service of worship. They listen when the Cross is upheld. But they do weary, and well they may, when "another gospel" is preached, for the Cross alone can satisfy the hunger of the soul.

# 24

## True Drawing Force
### *March 30, 1893*

THE masses of the people are not in the church, and to get them there is of the first importance. Under the stress to do something, many ingenious expedients have been devised and adopted. At times some of these expedients are successful in drawing crowds to the church. The main objection is that the spiritual force of the service must be lowered to get the people there, and still further depraved to hold them there. The crowds who are drawn by an appeal to itching ears, by sensational methods, must have their itchings gratified or else they will not come again. The crowds who flocked to Christ for the loaves and fishes or those affected by the sensation of his miracles were blown away like a breath when he laid "judgment to the line and righteousness to the plummet." The preacher who adopts nonspiritual methods will find himself in bondage to those who come, feeling compelled to give them what they want, for he knows as well as they do that they come for no spiritual ends and that they have no taste for the serious things of religion.

The preacher who deals with people who attend his ministry as one who must give account to God, as one on whose hands the blood of souls may be found in that tremendous day, such a man will pause a long while before he adopts any methods to attract people to his ministry that will at any point tend to abate the saving force of that drawing. Must a man preach to empty benches, then? Must he spend his force on a few? There are many things worse than preaching to a small charge. Preaching to a small congregation may illustrate the highest virtues and may secure the largest results. There is not on earth a graver responsibility than that of preaching to a large crowd. It may be a barren ministry on a barren soul.

We are not apologists for laziness, though it may exist under the guise of spirituality or conservatism. We believe that earnest fidelity to God and souls would double many a congregation. We believe that sensational methods are often adopted as the substitutes for painstaking spiritual work and that the pulpit often strives by superficial and exciting methods to create an interest, which can only be truly generated by work outside of the pulpit. No kind of preparation for the pulpit can atone for the failure to meet the duties that are the preacher's during the times when he's not delivering a message. Fidelity in the study and in the pulpit cannot fill the breach made by lack of fidelity in the home or in personal contact with the people. Faithful pastoral work will fill the average church and fill it with material out of which the largest spiritual results can be secured, fill it with a congregation who have given themselves to the preacher for the highest ends.

The maxim of Scotland's greatest preacher that "a house-going preacher will make a churchgoing people," is true everywhere and always. The preacher who shepherds his flock by visiting the people regularly and persistently as their personal spiritual friend and guide will fill his church to its capacity or to the limits of the field. In addition to this, he will create a spiritual activity in his people, which is of greater importance than their mere churchgoing habits. He touches his people in ways that move them. He knows them personally and handles them in their most susceptible places, for the best work is hand-sewed; the ripest, richest fruit hand-gathered. The pastor goes where the people live. He binds them to him by the mightiest forces: those are in the heart of a Christly preacher. He is one of them, and his life's current mingles with theirs. His presence and frequent loving visits create an interest in religion and in the church at home, which is the seat of life and the source of influence. The interest thus created is contagious; neighbors feel it and are drawn by it. Their doors and hearts are opened to the man and ministry whose tender interest and brotherly sympathy have been noticed.

We believe that people fall away from our churches and from religion because of the neglect of pastoral care: the lack of the pastor's heart and the failure to do the pastor's work. We have emphasized and rewarded fine preaching and have made so much of showy, popular gifts and so little of the elements of a holy pastorate that the forces that draw and cement people have been lost in our ministry. We have substituted attractive pulpit talents for the powerful forces of a pastor who calls his sheep by their names, knows their sorrows, is with them in their homes, and gladly lays down his life for them. It is not necessary to put the sheep into the hands of a robber to destroy them. The stranger or the hireling—the heartless pastor or the one who has his eye on his salary or on his reputation—will do the killing as effectually, if more slowly.

God's work cannot be done at long range. God's people cannot be saved at arm's length. Close to the people, one of them in their homes, in their hearts, and in their lives, must he be who saves them. The people will fall away from shams, from professionals in religion. They may endure professionals in the theater to while away an hour, but in the things of God and the serious matters of eternity, they must have hearts, real hearts, earnest and glowing, hearts whose blood they feel warming and touching their own. The people will support and have confidence in the true man of God. A true man of God will draw them, and they will hear Christ gladly. A true, Christly church will draw the people, but they will fall away from a sham man or from a sham church, from a cold man or from a cold church, from a dead man or from a dead church.

# 25

## Pastoral Work
### *April 27, 1893*

WE cannot place too high an estimate on fidelity in the pulpit. Duty and the times demand from the pulpit fidelity to God's truth and fidelity to the conscience and soul of the hearer. We cannot place too high an estimate on fidelity outside of the pulpit, for fidelity in the pulpit is only half fidelity. The preacher who deals with the souls of his people in the pulpit only, scarcely deals with them at all. We need preachers who will deal with men outside of the pulpit, deal with them not simply as acquaintances but deal with them for God, with all kindness but with all serious directness. We need preachers who will take advantage of every opportunity, appointed or not. Our chances for heaven will be slim if we don't have our preachers out of the pulpit. If they only preach to us from the pulpit, then the devil will have a life lease on us. We need pastors who have a passion for souls, not simply to get them saved but to keep them saved; for it is a more difficult work to keep folks saved than to get them saved.

The church cannot be kept vigorous and pure without the pressure of the pastor's eye, the pastor's hand, and the pastor's authority. The only remedy for the many ills flowing into the church is to be found in the diligent and vigilant care of a firm pastor. Worldliness must be charged by the pulpit, but it cannot be cured unless the individual is dealt with outside of the pulpit. Debauched business ways cannot be rectified by an annual sensational sermon, a well-ordered campaign, or a terrific assault from the pulpit. Against the sins that are hidden under the guise of business the pulpit must wage war without ceasing and preach against them till the preaching ceases to be a sensation and becomes a matter of irritation and of conscience. Then the individual must be dealt with alone, shut in with God, his conscience, and his pastor. Loose discipline, which is bringing such untold evils into the church, cannot be corrected except by dealing with the offenders in private as well as in public. There is not an evil in the church that cannot be cured by a fearless, loving, and firm pastor, a pastor who will devote himself to dealing with and saving the individual and thus purifying the church.

It is one of the evils of these times that Satan has been allowed to disparage the work of the pastor. Satan does not fear the brilliant preacher. He will compromise the work and give the preacher full possession of his study and great ability and reputation in the pulpit, if he, as a pastor, will let the people alone. Satan is well content to let Paul be the preacher if Satan can be the pastor. All worldly influences, social customs, home life, bitter prejudices, and public sentiment have been armed against the pastor's true work, which suffers in contrast to the public and showy efforts of the pulpit. The pulpit as an intellectual and proud profession has disdained the lowly work of the pastor. The ostentatious work of dealing with a crowd has been allowed to belittle the dealing with the one, and the pastor's legitimate and great work has been dishonored by the name of drudgery. Proud hands and prouder hearts and big reputations cannot stoop and be soiled by drudgery and so Satan and the world have almost shamed this divine work out of existence.

The pastor's duties outside of the pulpit are severely taxing. It is hard work, lowly work, delicate work, unshowy work, but work that has an impact on God's kingdom and on the eternal weal of souls. It is taxing work but not drudgery. It is the highest form of work, requiring the highest virtues, the clearest head, and the richest heart. It is not feet work, in contrast with head work, but it is knee work, head work, and heart work; work "what might fill an angel's heart, and filled a Saviour's hands."

The pastor's work requires time—a good deal of time. He can afford to give time to it. A successful pastor needs tenderness, patience, self-denial, and vigilance to watch over men. It requires love, like Christ's love, to shepherd men. Laziness and ease have no place in the pastor's consuming zeal. The good pastor will know his sheep, know their names and their sorrows. Solicitude will keep his eye and heart open and make his steps eager, his eye moist, his heart soft. Deep concern will mark and follow his sheep's wanderings and bring them back with all the sweetly compelling force of love. The good shepherd gives his life for the sheep. A man is worth more than a sheep, and the good pastor will give more than his life, if more he can give, for his sheep.

# 26

# Preaching to the Times
## *May 11, 1893*

Times like our own, rich in material advance and opportunity
with calls for all kinds of reforms, advances, and philanthropies
have a most fascinating effect on gifts, genius, sensation, or
ambition in the pulpit. It is a strong temptation for preachers
to strike the popular heart on the popular side. The themes
are fresh, alive, and attractive. Beside these present, agitating,
living issues, the doctrines and subjects of the Bible seem tame
and may strike on deaf ears and on irresponsive chords. The
interests of eternity don't seem as exciting as the spiced, stimulating subjects that concern this life.

For the pulpit to fall into this wave and preach to the times
and not from the Bible is fatal to faith and godliness. Enthu-
siasm may be quickened by such a course, reforms may flourish, and politics be improved, but faith will drag and the gospel
perish at heart. The falling away of the people from the church
in our great cities, the paganism and papalizing of New England
may in a great measure be traced "to the preaching up the
times." Archbishop Leighton, the pattern of holiness and of
pastoral efficiency, was publicly reprimanded for not "preaching up the times." "Who," he asked, "does preach up the
times?" The answer was made, "that all the brethren did it."

"Then," he replied, "if all of you preach up the times, you may allow one poor brother to preach up Christ Jesus and eternity." It seems to us that Leighton was following the example of Christ and his apostles who lived in peculiarly exciting times, but who ignored the times and rose above their short-lived and exciting interests and concerned themselves with the enduring and eternal. John the Baptist might have stirred the nation by preaching the popular and stirring themes of his times rather than the solemn and old-fogy doctrine of repentance; by so doing he might have escaped imprisonment and being buried by an apostate nation and an adulterous king in tears, but he would never have been the divine forerunner and herald of the Son of God.

The times of the French Revolution were times of great excitement in England. Adam Clarke was a man capable of handling governmental schemes and a true patriot; but while the pulpit and platform of England were rife with discussing the times, this great preacher would not yield to the popular demands. His biographer says:

> The French Revolution was the universal topic, and various political questions were agitated with considerable excitement. These were sometimes introduced into the pulpit, but by Mr. Clarke never; he informed me that during this painful period in almost every sermon he urged his hearers to seek entire sanctification.

It seems to us that Leighton and Clarke are in accord with the example of Christ and his apostles and in accord with the interests of true religion. Their methods are calculated to make the gospel more authoritative and attractive and aggressive than the way of preaching to the times though they will never be so popular, fresh, and delusively successful.

The congregation must feel that the preacher is above them, inhabits a more heavenly region, breathes a purer atmosphere, and it is disciplined by the effort to be by his side and share the riches of grace with which he is familiar. The preacher who would discipline others must discipline himself. His life must be chastened and subject. He must be an embodiment of the Sermon on the Mount, the thirteenth chapter of First Corinthians, and the "General Rules." His example, in order to be discipline, must be positive, commanding, firm, and erect. It must stand out clear-cut like the sphinx in the desert, thoroughly loyal to God and his truth without variableness or shadow of turning. His must be a life not to be contradicted or questioned, always declaring its Christly affinities and Christly spirit, always showing its brightness and heavenliness; always asserting its citizenship to the skies, no hair-splitting scales are needed to tell whether he belongs to earth or to heaven, whether he is for God or on the fence. His example must be so distinct that a blind man can see it, so strong that a stony man can feel it.

It is to be impressed on us that it is not smart sayings, it is not profound or original thoughts, or what the world thinks about the gospel or its preachers, but holy living, which is to make its impression on the world and train a church to a militant attitude for God. In the true idea of preaching, the preacher who lives better than anybody else will preach better than anybody else. The preacher's true power lies in what he is himself and what he lives, as well as what he preaches. The measure of the preacher's personal holiness will be the measure of his authority to shape his people for heaven. Holy, authoritative examples are needed everywhere. These are the true epistles and apostles of Christ. Nowhere are the apostles of holy living more needed than in the pulpit, which can be all-powerful and shine like a bright star. How dark, dull, and dead the pulpit that shines not with the luster of a holy life!

The preacher is bound to be an example in all things. He is bound to live the gospel, the whole gospel, as well as to preach it. He who does not live it cannot preach it. His words, though angelic, will be but sounding brass and tinkling cymbal. His church will be a demoralized, untrained army, the prey of every enemy. The gospel never looks so good, never sounds so good, and never fares so well as when coming out of the preacher's life. Then his words have weight and his life trains better than a manual of arms and a drill sergeant. Each word weighs a pound when impelled by the force of a holy life. Each sermon is a most terrific assault on sin and the world because it is backed by a life that has crucified sin and the world. The preacher's holy life is not only the great factory for saints but the successful training school for saintly soldiers.

# 27

## Severe Preaching
### *August 17, 1893*

PREACHING may be severe because the preacher is bad-tempered, harsh, and rough. If the severity proceeds from bad temper or from rough language, the preacher ought to get rid of his bad spirit, temper his bad words, or quit the pulpit. Preaching may be pronounced severe when the severity is in the condition of the hearer, and not in the spirit, manner, or words of the preacher. The sun might be adjudged unkind and intolerably severe on a sore place. The sun is a blessed thing; but diseased conditions turn the good and the blessed into instruments of torture. The Word of God is a blessed and kind thing when the conditions to receive it are right. It is like a fire and a hammer, though; it burns and breaks. It is a solvent, a searcher, a revealer. It is sharper than a two-edged sword, piercing to the dividing asunder of the joints and marrow and is a discerner of the thoughts and intents of the heart.

The quietness and harmony of many a congregation is nothing but the quiet harmony of death. A dead orthodoxy; a complaisant, politic worldliness; a pulpit without the unction of God's Spirit will have no friction because the graveyard inhabitants never get into conflicts.

Christ and Paul might have been, and doubtless were, charged with being severe preachers, but the severity was in the conditions and not in them. I was at one time in a place where the Word of God was creating a ferment and a conflict with certain sections of the church. I got out of the air of the friction and visited a desolate widow of piety and intelligence, and I felt like apologizing to her for the seeming sharpness of my preaching, but did not. After reading and praying with her, she said: "I want to thank you for the good your sermons are doing me." I saw in a moment that with her the conditions were so perfect that what some of my officiary and leading ones deemed severe came to her like the sun with its sweet, flooding light on a sound eye.

I was preaching at one time, and there came into the rear of the congregation a lawyer who is now the leading politician of his state. I was intent on preaching to the church members and only glanced at him enough to discern his intentness. He told his law partner that he felt like he was in hellfire up to his armpits during the whole of the sermon, and yet the sermon was a mild one, without, I think, one reference to hell. He was a sinner of the worst type, and the Word of God had set on fire the hell that was in him.

I remember well going into the pulpit with my spirit bathed with contrition and heartbrokenness, and my eyes could not exhaust the floods of tenderness and tears, and, under the power of the Spirit, I gave the Word of God. The next day I met the leading officiary of our church, reputed by us and by others to be among the best men in the city, if not the best. He attacked me most furiously and in the most violent temper. I did not recover from the shock for months. Afterward, when his conduct and spirit were revealed to me by those behind the curtains who knew the secrets of his temper and life, the whole mystery was explained. The severe conditions were in him, and the Word of God had probed the covered but festering sore.

While preaching a series of sermons in a protracted meeting, the leading and most efficient officer in the church, my warm personal friend, said to me, "You are preaching too severely to us; give us a sermon from 'God so loved the world.'" I thought and prayed over it, and determined to do it, if that were the right thing. In the midst of my perplexity and indecision I passed by his home, and his wife called me in and made known the secret burden of her heart, the intolerable sins of her husband, his badness of temper, and other things.

Those facts are to illustrate the principles laid down in this article.

Nothing can be further from the Spirit of Christ, no sin greater, than for a preacher to take advantage of his position to scold and abuse; but often that which is charged to the severity of the preaching is only the fearless spiritual preaching of God's Word falling on consciences diseased and inflamed, with the divine knife exposing their sore. These people remain in a continual state of irritation by refusing the remedy.

# 28

# Sincerity in Preaching
## *August 17, 1893*

THE preacher, of all men, ought to be a real man, a true man. Sincerity is the very life of the real and the true. Sincere, in its origin, means without wax, the pure strained honey—the pure thing without admiration. Sincerity is not exactly heartiness, but it is that to which heartiness owes its being. Sincerity combines reality of conviction and earnestness of purpose with purity. The pulpit needs sincere men. The great Puritan, John Howe, says he prayed that he might do the proper thing, but he prayed the more importunately that he might be sincere. Mistakes God would pardon, but no performance of duty that lacked sincerity could be acceptable to God. Insincerity not only destroys the efficiency and acceptability of every service but renders that service sinful. The following we reproduce as illustrative:

It is related that when Joseph Hume, the infidel, was taxed with inconsistency on going to listen to John Brown, the godly Scotch minister of Haddington, he replied:

"I don't believe all he says, but he does, and once a week I like to hear a man who believes what he says. Why, whatever I think, that man preaches as though he thought the Lord Jesus Christ were at his elbow."

There is a story of a couple of gentlemen who stopped at an out-door meeting in Scotland and listened while someone delivered an elegant and polished address.

"What do you think of that?" said one of them to his fellow.

"I think the man does not believe a word he says," was the reply.

After the first speaker had concluded, John Brown, of Haddington, rose up to preach, and poured out "the rivers of living water" which were welling within his own soul.

"And what do you think of that man?" said the traveler to his companion.

"Think," said he, "I don't know what to think. It seemed as if he thought Jesus Christ was standing by his side, and every little while he was saying, 'Now, Lord, what shall I say next?'"

Of Edward Payson, his biographer says:

Next to his prayers, the undoubted sincerity of his belief in the truths which he inculcated, was the cause of his distinguished and almost uninterrupted success. His language, his conversation and whole deportment were such as brought home and fastened on the minds of his hearers that he believed and therefore spoke. Though he drew crowds, there was nothing of stage effect—no imposing attitudes, no extremes of interruption, no affectation of tears. It was simple nature sanctified by grace, uttering the deep convictions of his heart!

The whole round of sensational preaching is a pestilential brood springing from an insincere pulpit. All pulpit performance, the mere acting a part, flows from the same source. The desire for place creates insincerity by bringing in wrong motives to influence. A preacher cannot think of place or salary without taint. The thought of these things destroys the singleness of eye. We need earnest men, but lack of earnestness belies sincerity. We need self-denying men, but lack of self-denial belies sincerity. We need brave men, but lack of strength belies sincerity. We need holy men, but sincerity is the foundation of holiness. The lack of this sincerity always cripples the ministry. God is served, but the motives are mixed. Insincerity divides or rots the service

# 29

## Good Hearers
### *August 31, 1893*

To be a good listener gives great satisfaction to the speaker and evinces qualities of a high order in the hearer. Docility, patience, self-restraint, and respect are some of the qualities of a good listener. The gospel is to be propagated by speaking. Its foundation principle, faith, comes by learning, and all its after and higher graces owe much of their growth to the art of good hearing.

The good hearer has a trained ear, an ear that has learned the salutary lesson of discriminating between the things it ought to hear and those it ought not to hear. It weighs words and tries them. Christ emphasized two statements. The first was, "take heed how you hear." He made the manner of hearing important. The thoughtful reverence, the devout receptivity of the hearing are all important. The second statement he emphasized was "take heed what you hear." The good hearer does not make his ears the dumping place for all the spiritual and doctrinal garbage that so called preaching may be pleased to unload. To hear wrong things is as damaging as to hear the right thing in a wrong way. Wrong words eat, says the Apostle, like a cancer. The good hearer has learned to hear the right thing in the right way.

The good hearer is swift to hear; that is, he is not dull or drowsy but on the alert, all ears to hear. Not a few church members and some leading ones are in the habit of going to sleep as soon as they get comfortably seated and the noise and excitement of the choir subsides and they are through with handing the collection-basket around. They certainly violate the apostolic injunction to be "swift to hear." Their dormant condition in the presence of God's word and their lack of interest ought to sober them to their true condition. The good hearer hears the word with meekness. This is a quality that destroys self-sufficiency, criticism, hardness, and all the tribe of self-inflated indocile qualities.

It is recorded of the Bereans that they received the word "with all gladness of mind." They had taste for and spirit in it. They were inclined and prepared to hear. They were good hearers and got good out of the preaching. There must be no impure food, indigestible or poisoned, given out of the pulpit; but the benefits of the preaching and the growth and vigor of spiritual life depend as much on the good qualities of the hearing as on the good qualities of the preaching—a bad digestion will turn honey to vinegar.

The good hearer will quicken his hearing by unloading his heart of all worldly cares. Christ declares that the cares of this world stupefy like intoxicants, which excite but then dull. The hearer, loaded down to the guards with the Sunday paper, will have leaden ears for God's truth and an iron heart.

The good hearer is a doer of the word. His weekday life is an application and reproduction of the last Sabbath sermon, and this gives him a good readiness for the next hearing. With him the sermon does not go in one ear and out at the other. With him the sermon is not a picture to be gazed at and admired; neither is it a nosegay to charm by its design or its odor. To him the sermon is solid food—angel's food. He feeds on it and grows strong.

The good hearer prays in secret before he goes to the church. A season of prayer and supplication fits his heart for the sermon and for all the reverent and devout attitudes of the house of God. Blessed are the good hearers. Whoever is in the pulpit is always fine with them in the pew. If the pulpit fails to feed, God feeds them on his chosen food. A sanctuary and a sacrament they have with him.

# 30

# An Important Distinction
## *September 7, 1893*

WE must never lose sight of the distinction between sensational preaching and preaching that creates a sensation. Sensational preaching is that kind of preaching that labors to create a sensation, always in stage attitudes, dealing in novelties, surprises, and any methods and devices that will create a wave of excitement. If sensational preaching deals at all with solemn verities and divine truth it does so in such a way as to destroy its lasting effect. Sensational preaching deals with the surface principles and puts them in an exciting form.

Preaching which creates a sensation may be of the most quiet and least exciting kind. Christ created a sensation by his teachings and works and yet was ever trying to allay the sensation that might create an unhealthy atmosphere, unfavorable to the deep and permanent work he desired to do. Robert Hall says of John Wesley that the greatest marvel about him was that though he was the quietest of men he kept everything around him stirring. The presentation of the solemn truths of the gospel by a man baptized into their spirit will often create the greatest sensation.

It may do to cover up our lack of zeal by decrying earnestness and spiritual power as sensational. Nothing can be further removed from the spirit of the gospel than sensational preaching; always working on the sensations, sympathies, emotions, or the nerves. Such preaching depraves spiritual taste, creates itching ears, and turns the gospel into "sound and fury signifying nothing." While this is kept in mind we must not emasculate the gospel, tone it down to a tameness that makes it insipid and nauseates. Neither must it be trimmed and polished so as to be without point, as glittering as an icicle and as cold.

Paul's preaching before Felix was no sensational effort. Here was a serious, brave man putting on the conscience of his auditors the truths of righteousness, temperance, and a judgment to come. It created a sensation though. Before Agrippa, Paul had a scene, but it was of no stage effect or sensational manufacture. It was the calm and unstudied utterance of a true man inspired and burdened by the great interests involved.

Of sensational preaching we cannot hear too little. Of the preaching that creates a sensation—profound, alarming, spiritual—we cannot hear too much.

# 31

## Pointless Preaching
### *September 14, 1893*

TOO much care may be given to sermons as a literary or intellectual product. The strength of the cross may be dissolved and its point blunted by our wisdom of words. John Wesley said he dared not preach a fine sermon. In these times we need directness, simplicity, conscience-reaching, and conscience-hurting words. We need strong words and weighty words, which give the gospel a personal and convicting force; words, which will drive sin out of the person or the sinner out of the church; words, which search and sift and separate; words, which attract and repel; words, which will press sin into close quarters and then show it no quarter. The following illustrates how words can be brilliant but pointless:

> After one of Robert Hall's brilliant and masterly sermons on covetousness, one of his hearers, remarked, "An admirable sermon! Yet why was such a sermon preached! For probably not one person in the congregation, though it is not wanting in examples of the vice in question, would take the discourse as at all applicable to himself."

The sermon was perfect as an oration but sadly defective as a sermon. It did not search out the sin in its lurking and hidden places. It did not tear off with seeming rudeness the disguises under which sin shielded itself. The sin of covetousness was not exposed in its naked deformity to the startled conscience. John Foster says of this sermon and the justness of the hearer's criticism that

> the preacher had employed his whole force on the love of money as a pure and absolute principle, and no one will acknowledge to be, or indeed, is conscious of being, actuated by this pure and absolute principle, however tenacious of his money or insatiably grasping at more. The passion enslaves and befouls him under secondary and more plausible forms. He wishes to have the means of setting his family advantageously forward in the world. It is gratifying to be looked up to with the deference universally shown to wealth. There is much liability to hazard and losses, and it is prudent to be well provided. It would be a miserable thing to suffer penury in old age. Now, an invective against the love of money to be practically useful, would seize and expose it in all those modes of its operations under which it hides or palliates its true qualities and beguiles out of all self-suspicions the most desperate idolator of Mammon.

It is right here that the fine sermon fails. It does not search out in vain. It is too general, too oblique, too ornate. It is too fine and delicate and deals with the imagination, the sensibilities, the intellect, the taste, the memory, and not with the conscience. It pleases when it ought to convict, satisfies self when it ought to break the heart, brings sunshine when it ought to bring thunder and lightning. It brings the fragrance of roses when it ought to bring a caustic.

Some preaching is but pleasant folly and does not rise to the point of pointless brilliance. Mr. Spurgeon says:

> Painfully do I call to mind a deliverance, which was an inquiry as to whether an angel did descend and stir the pool at Bethesda, or whether it was an intermitting spring. Dying men and women were assembled to hear the way of salvation, and they were put off with such vanity as this.

Many sermons fail, not through brilliance or from folly but from being smooth bores. A sailor, fresh from a whaling expedition, on his return from church was queried, "You do not seem to have liked the sermon?" "Not much," he replied. "It was like a ship leaving for the whale-fishing, everything ship-shape—anchor, cordage, sails all right—but there were no harpoons on board!"

No execution is done by such sermons. They are without teeth. Many fail to make the point because they are too nice, too soft, too feminine.

# 32

## Fine Sermons
### *September 21, 1893*

THERE is no surer way of grieving God's spirit, getting rid of his influence, and lowering spiritual operations to zero, than by preaching fine sermons; sermons in which learning, taste, intellect, philosophy, and poetry combine to make the sermon complete. This preaching is popular, pleasing, impressive; but the essential spiritual force is lost. The impression made does not reach the region of the spiritual. Sometimes the sentiment prevails that the great ecclesiastical leaders ought to do this elegant preaching; the lesser lights can confine themselves to the homely task of spiritual preaching: They that cannot think may pray. They that cannot be scholars may be saints.

Paul was a leader and a scholar, and he preached with the simplicity of a child, with all tenderness, and not with the stiff stateliness of a great leader. He preached like he prayed, as a saint and an apostle, not as a great thinker nor a great scholar. He judged and discarded fine and cultured deliverances; Christ, he declared, sent him to preach the gospel, "not with wisdom of words, lest the cross of Christ should be made of none effect." In this he declares that fine preaching destroys the efficiency of the cross. The eye and mind are turned away from the gospel to the sermon, its ideas, pictures, and brilliance. The

cross is swallowed up and lost in the beautiful thoughts and
stimulating ideas about Christ and other things.

Paul appeals to his own course to strengthen his statements
against this fine sermonizing to which the Greeks were so
prone:

> And I, brethren, when I came to you, came not with excellency of
> speech or of wisdom, declaring unto you the testimony of God. For
> I determined not to know anything among you, save Jesus Christ,
> and him crucified. And I was with you in weakness, and in fear, and
> in much trembling. And my speech and my preaching was not with
> enticing words of man's wisdom, but in demonstration of the Spirit
> and of power.
>
> [1 Cor. 2:1–4]

He did not clothe the gospel in an intellectual, scholarly,
philosophical, or poetic garb. He did not stretch his great intellect to its tension and by it mold the gospel into a beautiful,
seasonable, and attractive system. He narrowed it down to one
point and told it with the honesty, directness, and simplicity
of a witness bearing testimony to what he had seen and felt.
He left it to the Holy Spirit to take care of the demonstration
and power in applying the truth.

This is to put the emphasis where Christ puts it: Preparation
and ability to preach are secured by spiritual illumination and
heart purity and not by mental grasp, philosophical acumen,
or studious research. The men who hope to lead a generation
to Christ by the mere force of intellect and the culture of scholarship will not only miss that object but will fail to get there
themselves. Christ declares the great secret of knowing the
things of God. God has hid these things, he says, "from the
wise and prudent, and hast revealed them unto babes."

This age, so full of intellectual stimulants and intellectual
pride, so full of eulogistic and stimulating thoughts about
Christ, need to learn anew this lesson of how to preach the
gospel so as to secure the Holy Ghost to demonstrate it. This
is not in the interest of idleness, slipshod preparation, or com-

monplace, inane deliverances. It means turning our study and preparation from literature to revelation, from self to Christ, from the head to the heart. It means, instead of soaking ourselves in the fine thoughts of men about Christ, saturating our heads and hearts most thoroughly with God's thoughts. It means to baptize our sermons in the closet more than in the study. To do this will tax the powers of application, tax strength and time; but it will make us scribes thoroughly instructed in the things of God's kingdom, enabling us to bring out of our treasury things new and old—the old with the freshness of the new, the new with the friendliness and familiarity of the old. Our sermons, then, instead of tickling the ear, will break the heart; instead of adding to our reputation, will add to Christ's glory. We will then send our hearers off to repent, to weep, to praise God, and not to praise the sermon or the preacher.

# 33

## Pastor and Preacher
### *September 26, 1893*

PASTORAL work and pulpit work are most intimately connected. They exert a mutual influence on each other. Pastoral care gives a double weight to the preacher's words. Dr. Theodore L. Cuyler says; "No minister who ceases to be a pastor can continue to preach with pertinency and unction." John Wesley says:

> By repeated experiments we learn that though a man preach like an angel he will neither collect nor preserve a society which is collected without visiting them from house to house. I know no branch of the pastoral office which is of greater importance than this. But it is so grievous to flesh and blood that I can prevail on few even of our preachers to undertake it.

Grievous as it is it must be done or the church will suffer incalculable harm. The church is dependent on faithful pastors as much as on vigorous preachers for its prosperity. Vigorous preaching cannot atone for the lack of pastoral fidelity.

The pastoral work cannot be done from the pulpit, though much of pulpit work may be done in the most efficient way by the pastor in the home. To preach well and to look after the individual members of the church and to know them in their homes requires labor diligent and untiring. But to this exhaustive toil we are committed by the most solemn obligations.

# 34

## Sermons That Hit
### *October 5, 1893*

SERMONS ought to have a mark to shoot at like the rifleman; that is, every sermon ought to have its end and be prepared to secure that end. Christ's sermons hit—always hit somebody. Sometimes they hit with convicting and convincing force that broke up the heart into sorrow and repentance. Sometimes they enraged and only induced bitterness, opposition, and hate. Always intended to save, they frequently repulsed rather than attracted.

It is related of Mr. Wesley that his first inquiry about his lay assistants was: "Is anybody convinced of sin by their preaching? Is anybody made mad by their preaching?" If both of these questions were answered in the negative, he removed the preacher to another place.

Smoothbore preaching found no tolerance with Mr. Wesley. It is the Word of God, though, that does the execution, not the temper nor heat of the preacher. The only heat that he should have is the fire of the Holy Ghost. The preacher cannot too well guard his own spirit. It must be long-suffering and gentle. The servant of God must not strive but be patient and gentle toward all men. But the preacher's patience must not degenerate into weakness, nor his gentleness into insipid softness. The first martyr, Stephen, was a heavenly minded man, full of the Holy

Ghost; but his words went like chained lightning to the consciences of his hearers and cut them to the heart, and they gnashed on him with their teeth. His sermon was aimed at a mark and hit the center.

The sweetest-spirited sermon may provoke the bitterest opposition. The Word of God is not a negative quality, nor an edgeless force, but is sharper than any two-edged sword, piercing even to the dividing asunder of soul and spirit, and of the joints and marrow, and is a discerner of the thoughts, the intents of the heart. True preaching lays the heart and conscience bare and reveals sins as they will be exposed—naked—in the day of judgment.

All forms of sin and wickedness grow up and luxuriate under the eye and voice of preaching that never disturbs consciences nor awakens opposition. The preaching that has no repellent power will not have attractive force. The preaching that is not direct in its aim is a blank cartridge fired in the air.

# 35

## A Tearful Ministry
### *October 26, 1893*

To make people cry is no great spiritual gift. A sermon slush of tears may flow from many superficial causes. A crying preacher may be a very weak one, as well as a very strong one. The sentimental teardrop is paltry stuff. The "crying-to-order" preacher is a sham. While the Bible shows no favor to mere emotional or superficial conversions, it does make much of genuine heartfelt tears as the expression of godly sorrow, of true earnestness, of profound need. The Bible does make much of a tearful ministry—a ministry whose tears are the expression of profound convictions, deep solicitudes, tender sympathies, and deathless attachments. A tearless ministry never has saved and never can save the world. The stranger or the hireling shepherd can never fold and feed the sheep because they have no heart to weep over them. A tearful ministry is at a premium in the Bible; however, it may be discounted by our gospel of fun, which seeks to make people feel good and laugh heartily.

The true tearful element is a tender element full of compassion and sympathy, though not superficial. It belongs not simply to the eyes. It is not a sermon habit or a mere sermon effect. It impregnates the character and is one of its most marked elements. The whole career and character of the true preacher flows from the principle that he "goes forth weeping." What a charmed circle is around the statement, "Jesus wept!" What insight into his character that statement gives us! The gospel is there and his credentials to preach it as well. Humanity pauses at that and is won.

Tears have heat, warmth, and matchless charms. They are virtue's last defense, religion's last appeal. Religion has much use for tears. Its first lessons are learned by mourning hearts. It is our readiness to weep with those who weep that shows us to be Christian indeed. The ministers of such a religion must know full well the lessons that can be learned only by broken hearts and with tear-dimmed eyes.

A heartless ministry is the vicegerent of hell. These are heartless times, and no greater peril, no greater calamity can befall the ministry than to catch the contagion of these times. Many are the causes that conspire to dishearten the ministry. An iceberg is not less genial and life-giving than a heartless preacher, and tears are the sign of heart. It is said by one who knew "that it was the spirit of tender-hearted sympathy, which often found its outflow in tears, which made Mr. Spurgeon such a power for good." No true, powerful pastorate has ever been a fearless one. God's Hebrew prophets were serious men—men of the tearful eye and of the tearful heart. Jeremiah was the proverbial weeping prophet who wanted his head to be water and his eyes a fountain of tears that he might weep day and night. Isaiah, the most gifted of them, said, "I will weep bitterly, labor not to comfort me." The minister is not to deal with a system or a church—he is neither a professor nor a priest—but he deals with men, and a tearful tenderness is the gift for the man-winning power.

The ministry of Christ was a tearful ministry. The summary of his ministry is drawn by the divine pen, "who in the days of his flesh, when he had offered up prayers and supplications with strong crying and tears." His ministry broke his heart as well as sacrificed his life. The true apostles of Christ, the bravest and the best, have ever been like their Lord, tearful men. They have followed in his footsteps "weeping, bearing precious seed," and all their songs and success have grown out of a soil that they have watered and fertilized by their tears.

Paul's ministry was tuned to this strain of tearful tenderness. "Serving the Lord with all humility of mind, and with many tears." "I ceased not to warn every one night and day with tears." His letters were inspired by hearty compassion and sorrow. "For out of much affliction and anguish of heart I wrote unto you with many tears." "I . . . tell you, even weeping, that they are the enemies of the cross of Christ." His strongest and sharpest utterances were softened and bathed in tears. Timothy's ministry was one of tears: tears that touched Paul and gave intensity and charm to Timothy and his ministry.

Tears are the symbols and fruit of a compassionate ministry, a ministry that is one with the people, one with them in their burdens, griefs, sicknesses, and sins. Hearty, brotherly, tender, the tearful, Christlike minister is touched with a feeling of pity for the infirmities and trials of men. Sinful men, sorrowful men, imperiled men, weak men, strong men, all men need a tearful ministry. The bed of sickness and death are to be solaced, graves are to be covered with tears as well as with flowers, broken hearts are to be bound up with the oil of a new life. A preacher destitute of tenderness is as unfit for this ministry as unfitness can be. How we need to be in the company and school of Christ till our hearts are broken and we have caught somewhat of the sober seriousness, somewhat of the infinite tearfulness, somewhat of the fathomless sorrow that possessed him.

# Part Five

# 36

## A Rounded Ministry
### *January 11, 1894*

NEARLY every successful minister has his peculiar and easily recognized gifts. This is only to say that he possesses special adaptation for some particular kind or kinds of ministerial work and that he can do such work with better results than any other. It may be that he is a master in the pulpit, or that he is singularly skillful in the art of pastoral visiting, or that he excels in the capacity for organizing his congregation so as to put everybody to work and to get the largest outcome from the material at his disposal. That he should find his greatest enjoyment in the cultivation and exercise of his best faculties—whatever they may be—is a reasonable expectation. We assume it, as a truth beyond dispute, that the line of highest and most praiseworthy activity for any man is indicated by the specific character of his natural endowments.

It is also necessary, in order to avoid narrowness and one-sidedness, to give due heed to another consideration. Though a minister may appear at his very best in discharging one class of duties, it is still the fact that he cannot afford to neglect any duties that his office puts upon him. For example, even if he preach like Jeremy Taylor or George Whitefield, thrilling his auditors with his glowing words, he dare not say, "I have no time to be running from house to house, my business is in my study." The man who talks after this fashion betrays a woefully deficient conception of the pastoral office. Real pastoral visiting is not a mere gadding about, requiring the use of the legs but making no draft on the brains and the heart. It is, in fact, an intelligent approach to the people for the sole purpose of doing them good. At the same time, it is the best schooling for efficiency on the platform and in the pulpit to which one can be subjected. As we see it, there is no other way in which a man can thoroughly acquire that genuine human sympathy, which is an indispensable element of power in a public speaker. Incessant and unrelieved intimacy with books withers up the sensibilities of the soul. All knowledge is dead until it is vitalized by actual contact with human life. Many things are learned among men that can never be learned in the seclusion of the library. The world itself is a great university in which lessons of incalculable value are taught. We insist, therefore, that the hours that are spent about the firesides of the people in close, familiar, and earnest conversation and in devout prayer, instead of being a subtraction from the completeness of one's public discourses, are a reinforcement and addition to them. No time for pastoral visiting! The plea is absurd. An astronomer might as well urge that he is so engrossed with books and charts as to have no time for the telescopic investigation of the actual heavens.

On the other hand, it is equally important for the minister of distinguished social gifts, who relishes his outings among the members of his flock better than the exacting tasks of reading, writing, thinking, and prayer, to bear in mind that he is exposed to a serious danger. Unless he keeps a careful watch over himself and religiously attends to the mastering of his books and to the preparation of his sermons, he will presently discover that nobody cares to see him. The empty-headed babbler, who gets up on Sunday after Sunday only to let his tongue wag without saying anything, is not a welcome guest in all homes. This honor is reserved for the diligent student who in the Lord's house always has a message and brings forth out of his treasure things new and old for the edification of his hearers. And it is right that it should be so. There is positively no excuse for the vacuity, the dullness, the lack of thought, and the absence of power that characterize the utterances of some ministers. Why should there be any desire to see on Monday the negligent preacher who wanted the glorious opportunities of the Sabbath and sent home two hundred or five hundred men and women, after an hour's tedious talk, without having given a single fresh suggestion to their minds or kindled a single fresh aspiration in their hearts?

Old men are set in their ways, and to them I do not write. At the utmost I have scant hope of getting them to lay aside their bad habits and adopt good ones. But I do address myself with special urgency to our younger brothers, who are just now entering upon their high calling. If they are wise, they will seek from the beginning to show themselves workmen that need not be ashamed in respect to every obligation, great and small, connected with their ministry. They will find time enough to do everything that ought to be done, provided they have common sense enough and energy to use instead of abusing their opportunities. The world laughs—when it does not sneer—at the man who in any vocation is perpetually talking about what marvels he would accomplish, if he could only get a little time. In every day there are 24 hours, and in every year 365 days. What more can anyone ask?

# 37

## Put Salt in It
### *February 1, 1894*

REAL preaching "is quick, and powerful, and sharper than any two-edged sword, piercing even to the dividing asunder of soul and spirit, and of the joints and marrow, and is a discerner of the thoughts and intents of the heart" (Heb. 4:12). Real preaching deals with men's consciences and men's sins. In its dealing it is personal and direct. It rebukes, reproves, exhorts, and has some of the fiery inquisition of the Judge. It is clothed with some of the scrutiny and terrors of the judgment. It opens the books before the thrones are set and arraigns and alarms before the trumpet calls. Preaching of this kind is a salty preaching. It is felt. Men dread a pulpit of this kind, for it causes public sentiment. It maintains the authority of God. It demands a hearing. It is powerful. Sin and Satan are cowardly, but they do not retreat until they meet courage. They must be rebuked before they retire in shame.

Preaching that has no salt in it is not the preaching for the present day. Salt is pungent, salt penetrates, salt gives relish; it saves from insipidity as well as from corruption. Without the salty qualities preaching neither penetrates nor saves. These times are too strenuous to be arrested by saltless preaching. Salt finds the sore and makes it smart. The great facts of God's revealed Word are the salt, and the preacher is to put the salt in contact with the world's corruptness. He must put the salt in thick layers and with a smarting application.

It is appalling to think of the many forms of worldliness and sin that flourish under the eye and voice of many a modern pulpit. It would often seem that the pulpit had no mission to save—only to please and to entertain. The function of the pulpit to search and alarm consciences seems a lost function. The world, self-satisfied, without shame or blush, sits in its cushioned pew. Popular sins luxuriate among the church officials, and the pulpit seems to have no mission to bring conviction and salvation, or even to make these sinners in Zion afraid.

Something must be done. All forms of worldliness and many forms of sin are in our pews. The sins of indifference and sloth are there. The sins of selfishness, ease, indulgence, pride, dishonesty, covetousness, avarice, intemperance, and passion breed and swarm in our pews like insect life in the beams of the sun. Worldliness in myriad forms grows and luxuriates in the warmth of church air. The low tone of spiritual life and its lukewarmness take the savor out of church life, and corruptions multiply without restraint. Salty preaching is the only cure for this condition. Sin is to be rebuked, the world is to be denounced and renounced, consciences are to be made and aroused, a high-toned public sentiment is to be created. To do this the pulpit must be personal and pungent. The preacher who aims to do this without pungency is as far out of the way as he who undertakes to fashion iron without the fire.

There can be no truer statement than that salt was a prominent ingredient in the preaching of Jesus. If his preaching was not salty it was nothing. We are at a loss to determine which quality of his was greater: tender concern for men or fidelity in dealing with them. The elements of tenderness and pungency are not antagonistic but are coexistent in true character. Bitterness and sharpness are not the same. Bitterness is sharpness with the fire of passion in it. Sharpness is fidelity and truth on edge. Sharpness is purity with its whip of cords used and

made vehement by a holy zeal for Christ and a holy indigna-
tion against shameless sacrilege and churchly dishonesty and
worldliness.

The salt must be put in, not with bitterness but with tenderness. The salt need not be driven in with a sledge hammer,
and the skin doesn't need to be torn off to apply it. It is salt
that has the savor, and that salt must be put in. Sell out your
sugar and buy salt. Strike out the poetry from your sermons
and put in red hot, homely, hard truth—truth that is rough
enough to be strong and leave its smart, too strong for rhythm.
There was neither sugar nor poetry in Paul's description of the
Cretians: "Always liars, evil beasts, slow bellies;" nor in Christ's
pronouncement to the Pharisees: "Ye serpents, ye generation
of vipers, how can ye escape the damnation of hell?"

# 38

## Popularity
### *April 19, 1894*

INFLUENCE and popularity are very different. Influence is the power that flows out from a man. Popularity is the applause of the people, coming from outside the man. There may be great influence and little popularity. There may be no influence and great popularity. Influence is abiding. Popularity comes and goes. A preacher may be very popular without seeking it. To be indifferent to it is a great grace. To seek it is a great sin. Popularity feeds pride. "If we had no pride," said a holy preacher, "I believe applause would give us no pleasure."

In his diary Robert McCheyne makes this record in regard to a preacher: "Mr. _____ died this morning at 7:00. O that I may take warning, lest after preaching to others, I myself be cast away. Love of popularity is said to have been his besetting sin." During a sickness, which laid him aside, Mr. McCheyne occupied himself with finding out the plagues and secret sins of his heart, and he made this record of his discovery: "I have been too anxious to do great things. The lust of praise has ever been my besetting sin." Popularity and praise are sweet but siren voices. The good preacher is often shorn of his power by his people glorying in him. God had often to make Paul unpopular that his ministry might not fail. The preacher must shut his ears to popularity for there is no more dangerous thing than popularity, no more unstable thing to a true man. The love of popularity causes one to surrender convictions and debauch character. Seeking popularity is deceptive. It is seeking self in the form of seeking good.

When the preacher begins to follow after the popular waves, when the voice of applause has become sweet to him, he has entered on the road of apostasy. He had better be with his Master in Gethsemane in agony and alone or with him without the camp bearing his reproach than with the crowd. Weakness may yield to the rush and clamor of popular demands because it lacks firmness or courage to resist; but to seek the popular tide, to find out the public sentiment before we speak, destroys manliness and religion.

The gospel does not follow popular channels. To it the demagogue cry that "the voice of the people is the voice of God" is profane. Duty and conscience must stem wind and tide. The current of public sentiment must be breasted by the advocate and preacher of the gospel. Unpopular measures must be championed and unpleasant crosses borne by the true Christian. The gospel is not to be the minister for self to preachers or to hearers. This is an unpopular system for it crosses popular waves and defies public sentiment. Transformed, and not conformed, is the first law of its unpopular but divine life.

The examples from McCheyne's diary are illustrative and warning. McCheyne and the preacher whose death he notes had the same besetting sin. The one saw it, encouraged it, yielded to it, and was lost. McCheyne saw how pleasing popularity was to him and how ensnaring; he fought against it. In his alarm and piety he conquered it and made his way to heaven. Safety and salvation are not found in the difference in our native goodness or badness, not in the strength or weakness of our fleshly tendencies, but in the courageous, persistent fight we are making against these tendencies and the invincible and triumphant nature of that fight. We become good by fighting the evil in us. The best we can do is to get good and be good. Our first and too often last fight for heaven is with ourselves. The next fight is against the things that please us most and which lie near us.

# 39

# Demands on the Pulpit

## *April 26, 1894*

THE demands for the enlargement of the sphere of the pulpit to save it from decline and add to its efficiency are delusive and damaging. The Hebrew prophets shook the Hebrew nation. The Christian pulpit has a sphere large enough to shake the Christian nations. The salvation of ancient Israel came out of Zion. The permanent prosperity of the Christian nation depends on the purity and prevalence of religion. The purity and prevalence of religion depend on the spiritual vigor of the pulpit. The pulpit needs no widening of its sphere. It only needs to fill its sphere with efficiency and fidelity.

The pulpit must keep the fact and enormity of sin alive. The pulpit is charged by the gravest considerations to emphasize the existence, guilt, and ruin of sin. The gospel has no force nor meaning, its Christ no mission, but from the fact of sin. Sin colors man's thoughts and gives bent to his nature. It is the mystery of mysteries and is the woe that drapes earth in sorrow. Sin is earth's great shame. Its effects and ruin are appalling. It is so sad and shameful that we are ever prone to forget or ignore its existence. It is the devil's great wile to hide sin from our eyes. He commissions everything—philosophy, literature, public sentiment, religion—to deny or hide the fact of sin, but the pulpit is armed with the power and charged with the responsibility of keeping the fact of sin alive in the conscience of men. If the pulpit fails to awaken to the fact and evil of sin, its gospel is a physician without a patient, a remedy without a disease. The idea of sin must be kept conspicuous and vivid. Its existence must not degenerate into mere sentiment nor its presence relieved by delusive ideas, as flowers relieve the coffin. No pernicious views of the fatherhood of God and no illusive poetry of an eternal hope must be allowed to ensure and blind the conscience to the appalling fact and dire results of sin. How the early Methodist pulpit in its mighty conquering force stressed sin and its ruinous effects! They put sin in the very bone of man's being and drew appalling pictures of its ravages and eternal ruin. We are too well bred to offend by such ill-bred ideas.

Emphasizing sin, its exposure and conviction, demands that the pulpit deal with law, not the law of Moses but the law spiritualized by Christ and made efficient by the Holy Ghost. This is the dispensation of the Spirit, but the dispensation of the Spirit exerts its full force to "reprove the world of sin, and of righteousness, and of judgment." This is law—the law of the Spirit. Felix wanted to hear from Paul about Christ and he did hear of him through "righteousness, temperance, and judgment to come." This is law—the law of Christ. The utterances of the pulpit must often be legal, for by the law is the knowledge of sin. The law is God's straightedge—the crooks and rents of sin are discovered by it. The law lays the claim of God on the conscience. It demands a perfect righteousness in heart and life. This age, in its rapacity, in its intoxication and disquiet, cannot be arrested and sobered but by the restraining and inexorable demand of law. A stronger hand must lay hold of the mighty defiant forces that enslave men. Our lax lawlessness must have law for the conscience, law for the heart, law for the life. The law of righteousness must go hand in hand with the law of faith. The crying need of these times is for the pulpit to lay "judgment . . . to the line and righteousness to the plummet." It must be taught that there is much more in religion than the antinomian cry, "life for a look."

The legal functions of the prophet belong to the New Testament preacher. Its exercise will be most beneficial. Consciences are made and quickened by law. The Sermon on the Mount has more of searching flame and searching law in it than the Ten Commandments. An infusion of the law from Tabor and Sinai is what this age needs. The Sermon on the Mount and the Ten Commandments ought to be written by the pulpit in letters of fire on the business life, home life, and church life. The elements of our civilization are so heterogeneous, so strenuous, and its results are so grasping, so deadening that nothing short of law can break its mastery.

The preaching of law means to declare the penalty. In view of the trend of things it is not out of place to ask, has the law any penalty? If so, what is it? The pulpit ought to answer that question in every sermon. Law without a penalty is worse than trifling, and insult to conscience and to judgment. The modern idea ignores law and despises its penalty. The only solution of the expense and mystery of Christ's life and death is the inexorable and infinite demands of God's law, the inexorable and fearful penalty to which its violators are exposed. No prophet was ever more vigorous for law than Christ. No prophet, apostle, or preacher ever painted in more appalling terms the penalty of that law. In the teaching of Christ the penalty of the law not only meets the guilty and impenitent at every point to warn of peril and of loss, but the certainty and dread of the penalty are ever kept before the disciple as an incentive to the most painful self-denial and the most exhaustive effort. It is used to quicken fear, to increase benevolence, and to incite to mercy. All the virtues to be obtained, all the rewards to be secured, are enhanced and edged by reminders and pictures of the doom of the lawless.

The pulpit, if true to its designs, should be urgent and sleepless in its efforts to awaken men to the fact and penalty of sin. These should make the pulpit serious, weighty, earnest.

Statement and argument, fact and reason should be marshaled to arouse and impress. Imagination, if not fancy, has its province here. The reproduction of Christ's awful picture of the eternal separation of the good and bad, with the trembling and despairing crowd on the left waved off and consigned to the eternal flames, has its uses. The bald facts justify all attempts to arouse and make even extravagance sober. Nothing is so alarming as to see the pulpit turning into the green and quiet shades of literature, losing itself in the intricacies of critical or scholarly love, or becoming drowsy, dull, self-indulgent entertainment mongers when issues so vital and claims so urgent and deathless are imminent.

There is no institution with more power to create a healthy sentiment and to usher in the reign of righteousness than a pulpit true to its divine design. It is the banner of virtue, a protest and a menace to evil and evildoers. There is a no more despicable and demoralizing thing than a pulpit with surface views of sin and responsibility, tame and veering, without God, without conscience, without law. A fool's errand is the sum of wisdom compared to such an institution. Whatever weak and sentimental ideas in regard to sin may prevail and poison literature, philosophy, or theology, the pulpit must be nerved by a vigorous faith and must hold to the divine statement of sin and sinfulness, the inflexibility of God's law, and the certainty and severity of its penalty. The whole counsel of God must be declared, or else soul bloodguiltiness will stain the pulpit.

# 40

## Compliments
### *May 3, 1894*

LUTHER never spoke a truer word than when he said, "In truth I see and feel that those who mention me to my disadvantage do me most good." Happy are the ways of an enemy to a man seeking to perfect himself in virtue or religion for an enemy never flatters, and that is a great and good thing.

Compliment is the synonym of adulation and flattery, but being the popular and active member of the firm it has absorbed to a great degree the capital, character, and uses of the others. Less offensive to taste, with a fairer reputation than either flattery or adulation, compliment gives currency and value to the worst features of both. It is not so sordid nor cringingly false as adulation, yet it keeps its eye open to the interests of number one and is always complaisant and obsequious if it ever speaks. Not so gross as flattery, it smooths its tongue, improves its taste, and flatters more wisely and more delicately than flattery could do. Compliment was born and christened in hardy times and started on an honest and manly career, but it went to school to policy; fell in company with insincerity, guile, and fashion; and lost its original simplicity and character, becoming the servant of selfishness and servility and not the friend of duty and high esteem.

The fear of being dull or uninteresting often leads to compliments. But the weak, unamiable, selfish desire to please is the fruitful source of this bad thing. Banter, lacking heart or head may be profuse in compliments. But complimenting is not always playful or heartless or headless. It is often a very deliberate and serious business, having method, head, and heart in it. The set purpose is to gain influence and to be popular. Complimenting is the route to that influence or popularity. Compliment is the ready slave of ambition. It is the demagogue's right hand. It does not "wade through slaughter to a throne," but it does that which in its measure is as criminal: It creates and inflames vanity. It destroys simplicity and purity. Of compliment Mr. Wesley said: "A vile word, the very sound of which I abhor. I advise men of sincerity and simplicity never to take that silly word into their mouths, but labor to keep at the utmost distance both from the name and the thing."

Vanity is the strong point of weak men and the weak point of strong men. Compliment comes in at the point of vanity. It is always a welcome visitor at the door. The exposure of women to attacks on the side of vanity is proverbial, but the proverb has been made by the vanity of man. Vanity may be hereditary with woman, with man it is epidemic and natural. Vanity is universal in the race, and to gratify it is the surest road to favor. Complimenting is the surest way to gratify vanity. That all men have a streak of vanity is true, and it makes one feel good to tickle this vanity, but it is not true that duty or piety demand us to minister to this vanity. It cannot be innocently ministered to. Our duty is to cure it, for it and piety cannot coexist. Roughness, sourness, and severity are not the antonyms or cure for complimenting. But honesty, fidelity, and plain, sober speaking are the remedies for its insincerity, falsehood, and its thousand other evils.

In God's language, to the stern old Hebrew, *flattery* means smooth. The false prophets did not bring God's message but prophesied smooth things because this pleased the people and made the prophets popular and influential. Many a modern pulpit seeks to bring not the message that God would have them bring but the message that pleases. With them, that blasphemous maxim prevails, "The voice of the people is the voice of God." In these pulpits smooth doctrine, oily sentences, and pleasing compliments have been the staple commodity so long that the people will not tolerate candor, sincerity, nor sound doctrine. The preacher who expects to do good by flattery puts on the devil's armor to fight God's battles and claims Christ's property with the devil's signature and seal. Paul declared that he flattered no man and that if he sought to please men he would not be the servant of Christ.